Mnemonic

devised by
the Company

D0067266

Methuen Drama

Methuen

3 5 7 9 10 8 6 4

First published in Great Britain in 1999 by Methuen Publishing Limited
215 Vauxhall Bridge Road, London SW1V 1EJ

This revised version published in 2001

Copyright © 1999, 2001 Complicite
Photographs copyright © Sebastian Hoppe 1999

The right of Complicite to be identified as the author of this work
has been asserted by them in accordance with the Copyright, Designs
and Patents Act, 1988

Methuen Publishing Limited Reg. No. 3543167

A CIP catalogue record for this book is available from the British Library

ISBN 0 413 74720 4

Typeset by SX Composing DTP, Rayleigh, Essex
Printed and bound in Great Britain by
Cox & Wyman Ltd, Reading, Berkshire

Caution

Complicite
Mnemonic

Conceived and Directed by	Simon McBurney
Originally Devised by	Katrin Cartlidge, Richard Katz, Simon McBurney, Tim McMullan, Stefan Metz, Kostas Philippoglou, Catherine Schaub Abkarian.

Director	Simon McBurney
Design	Michael Levine
Lighting	Paul Anderson
Sound	Christopher Shutt
Costume	Christina Cunningham

Cast	Katrin Cartlidge, Richard Katz, Simon McBurney, Tim McMullan, Kostas Philippoglou, Catherine Schaub Abkarian, Daniel Wahl

Production Manager	Rodger Hulley
Company Stage Manager	Anita Ashwick
Assistant Director	Steven Canny
Assistant Designer	Patrick Donohue
Assistant Sound Designer	Gareth Fry
Technical Stage Managers	Paul Hollingbery
	Rod Wilson
Puppet Designer-Maker	Simon Auton
Production Photography	Sebastian Hoppe

Originally a co-production with the Salzburg Festival.
This version opened at the Lyttelton Theatre on 2 February 2001.

The production runs 1 hour 55 minutes. There is no interval.

Complicite would like to thank the following for their help with this production: Annabel Arden, Battersea Arts Centre, Frank Baumbauer, Lilo Baur, Paul Bennun, John Berger, Will Bowen, Henrietta Butler, Carphone Warehouse, Annie Castledine, Guy Chapman Associates, Chris Chibnall, Anna Clayden, Creaseys, Dept. Radiology Aberdeen Royal Infirmary, Rebecca Fifield, Hannes Flaschberger, Kate Higginbottom, Renata Klett, Emma Laxton, Elena Lehmann, Lever Bros, Michael Meller, Anne Michaels, Mitch Mitchell, Nicky Pallot, Parsons, Polish Cultural Institute, Doug Rintoul, Regents Park Open Air Theatre, Scanner, Christiane Schneider, Sightlines, South Tyrolean Museum of Archaeology, lighting supplied by Sparks Theatrical Hire, Konrad Spindler, Steel the Scene, Polly Stokes, Professor Weir, Mark Wheatley, Young Vic Theatre, Peter Zander.

FOR COMPLICITE

Complicite is funded by The Arts Council of England and London Arts and is supported by The British Council. Registered Charity number 1012507.

SUPPORTING OUR FUTURE

Complicite is a Company that is artistically led using exploratory workshops to clarify its output. This process of development and experimentation has resulted in the Company's most successful, ground-breaking projects. We need your help to continue to produce work of this nature.

To support us, become a Friend of Complicite.
Send a cheque for £25 (£30 outside the UK) or £100 or £500 made payable to Theatre de Complicite to our address below. As a Friend you will receive newsletters, mailing list membership, advance booking for productions and ticket
and merchandise offers.

You involvement is of vital importance to us.

Complicite
14 Anglers Lane, Kentish Town, London NW5 3DE UK
Tel +44 (0)20 7485 7700 fax +44 (0)20 7485 7701
email@complicite.co.uk

Paul Anderson
Trained at Mountview Theatre School and York College of Arts and Technology. **For Complicite:** *Light, The Noise of Time, The Chairs* (nominated for Olivier, Drama Desk and Tony Awards). Relights for *The Street of Crocodiles, The Caucasian Chalk Circle, The Three Lives of Lucie Cabrol.* **Other design:** *A Servant to Two Masters* (RSC and West End); *As I Lay Dying, Twelfth Night, West Side Story, Guys and Dolls, Arabian Nights* (Young Vic); *Cinderella* (Theatre Royal Stratford East); *The Threesome, Pinocchio* (Lyric Hammersmith); *Special Occasions, Hospitality, A coupla' white chicks sitting around talking, Blue Window* (North America Theatre UK); *The Double Bass* (Man in the Moon); *The Christie Brown Exhibition* (Wapping Pumping Station); *Rediscovering Pompie* (IBM Exhibition).

Anita Ashwick
Trained at Central School of Speech and Drama. **For Complicite:** *The Noise of Time, Light, The Street of Crocodiles, The Caucasian Chalk Circle, The Three Lives of Lucie Cabrol.* **For the Young Vic:** 3 years as Company Stage Manager including *More Grimm Tales* in New York and Sydney. **Other theatre includes:** *Return to the*

Forbidden Planet (Drama City Theatre Japan), *Blood Wedding* (Womens Playhouse Trust), *When We Are Married* (Whitehall Theatre), *Light Up The Sky* (The Old Vic). **Opera:** *Cosi Fan Tutte, Yan Tan Tethera, Marriage of Figaro, Don Giovanni, Coronation of Poppea, The Rakes Progress* and *The Bacchae* (Opera Factory), *Ariadne Auf Naxosand Zaide* (The Orchestra of the Age of Enlightenment), *The Bartered Bride, Force of Destiny, Carmen, The Mikado, the Mask of Orpheus, The Queen of Spades* (English National Opera). Has also worked as a props buyer and for three years co ran a production services company and scenic workshop.

Steven Canny
For Complicite: *The Noise of Time, Light.* **Directing:** *Rabbit Punching, Burglar Beware,* (GriP Theatre); *An Act of Will* (British Council Tour and Edinburgh Festival). Winner of the John Fernald Award.
Other work: As script reader (theatre, film and television), theatre reviewer, musician and as an actor and technician on the fringe.

Katrin Cartlidge
Theatre: *Apart From George, The Terrible Voice of Satan* (Royal Court); *The Strangeness of Others, The Garden of England, Salome* (RNT); *The*

Present (Bush Theatre). **Film:** *Naked* (dir. Mike Leigh, Winner of the most promising European Actress award, Geneva '94); *Before The Rain* (dir. Milcho Manchevski); *Breaking the Waves* (dir, Lars Von Trier); *Career Girls* (dir. Mike Leigh, Winner Best Actress Evening Standard Film Awards '97); *Claire Dolan* (dir. Lodge Kerrigan; to be released: *From Hell* (dir. Alan & Albert Hughes); *No Man's Land* (dir. Danis Tanovic).

Christina Cunningham
Trained at Wimbledon School of Art. **For Complicite:** *Light, The Noise of Time, The Street of Crocodiles.* **Costume design:** *Prophet in Exile* (Chelsea Centre); *De Profundis, Just Not Fair* (RNT/Birmingham Rep); *Fire Raisers* (Riverside Studios). **Costume supervisor:** *The Misanthrope, Hurly Burly, Prayers of Sherkin* (Peter Hall Company); *Personals, The Boyfriend* (*Hey Mr Producer,* Lyceum); Moving Theatre's season at Riverside Studios.

Gareth Fry
Originally trained as a recording engineer and subsequently in theatre sound design. He works extensively in theatre and on site-specific events. **For Complicite:** *The Noise of Time, The Street of Crocodiles* (Tokyo, Stockholm and the West End). **Sound designs:**

The Country (Royal Court); *The Oresteia* (Royal National Theatre); *The Wexford Trilogy* (Tricycle Theatre); *Play to Win* (Soho Theatre). **Other work:** *The Cost of Living* (DV8 Physical Theatre); *Greenwich Meridian Clock* (Greenwich Festival); *Style of our Lives* (LIFT).

Paul Hollingbery
Studied at Cambridge, now working freelance within the theatre industry. **For Complicite:** *Light.* **Other work:** Automation at the Royal Opera House and for *The Witches of Eastwick* (Theatre Royal Drury Lane); *Eurydice* (Whitehall Theatre) and assorted events and conferences.

Richard Katz
Trained at Bretton Hall College. **Theatre:** *Arabian Nights* (Young Vic); *Cinderella* (Improbable Theatre/Lyric Hammersmith); *Don't Laugh it's My Life* (Told By An Idiot); *UBU ROI* (Gate); *Twelfth Night* (Imaginary Forces), *Wind in the Willows, The Skriker* (RNT); *In Savoy* (RNT Studio), *Much Ado About Nothing* (Queens); *The Games Rule* (Tandem Theatre at Waterman's Art Centre); *All God's Chillun Got Wings* (West Yorkshire Playhouse); *The Honest Whore* (606 Theatre at The Boulevard), *Sganerella* (USA Tour); *A Slight Accident, Rosencrantz and Guildenstern*

are Dead (European Tour).
Radio: Writer and performer of
The Newbury Arms (Radio 4).
TV: *The Life and Times of
Nicholas Nickleby, The Bill,
London's Burning, Finding
Freud.* **Film:** *Enigma, The Last
Sin.*

Michael Levine

Michael Levine has worked
internationally in theatre,
opera, dance and film.
Theatre: *A Midsummer Night's
Dream, Tectonic Plates* (RNT);
Revengers Tragedy (RSC);
*The Faust Project, The
Designated Mourner, Possible
Worlds, Marathan 33, Arms
and the Man, Heartbreak
House, The Women, Skin of
Our Teeth* (all in Canada), *The
Housekeeper, Torquato Tasso,
Impressario From Smyrna,
Custom of the Country* (Glas-
gow Citizens Theatre). **Opera:**
Dr. Ox's Experiment (ENO);
*Blue Beard's Castle,
Erwartung, Oedipus Rex, The
Symphony of Psalms* (Canadi-
an Opera Company) and pro-
ductions for The Metropolitan
Opera, Paris Opera,
Netherlands Opera, Vienna
State Opera, Welsh National
Opera, Festival D'aix,
Houston, Chicago and San
Francisco Opera, Washington
Opera and Santa Fe Opera.
Dance: *C'est Beau Cas*
(Dancemakers); *Hothouse*
(National Ballet of Canada0.
Film Projects: *September
Songs* (Rhombus Media).

Simon McBurney

Studied at Cambridge and
trained in Paris. Co-founder
and Artistic Director of
Complicite with whom he has
devised, directed and acted in
over 24 productions, toured all
over the world and won
numerous major international
awards. As a director he has
been nominated for Olivier,
Drama Desk and Tony Awards.
Most recently he directed *Light*
and conceived and directed
The Noise of Time, commis-
sioned by the Lincoln Centre,
New York and performed with
the Emerson String Quartet.
As an actor Simon has performed extensively for radio,
television and film including
*Sleepy Hollow, Kafka, Tom and
Viv, Being Human, Mesmer,
The Ogre, Cousin Bette,
Onegin.* To be released:
Eisenstein, Morality Play.

Tim McMullan

Trained at RADA. **For
Complicite:** *Light, The Noise
of Time, In the Dark, To The
Wedding* (BBC Radio 3), *The
Caucasian Chalk Circle, The
Three Lives of Lucie Cabrol.*
Other theatre: *Racing Demon,
Wind in the Willows, The Miser,
The Resistible Rise of Arturo
Ui, Murmuring Judges, Richard
III* (RNT); *Arabian Nights*
(Young Vic); *The Front Page*
(Donmar Warehouse); *The
Merchant of Venice* (Sheffield
Crucible); *The Tower*
(Almeida); *Mirandolina* (Lyric

Theatre); *Lady Betty* (Cheek By Jowl); *Road* (Wolsey Theatre); *She's in Your Hands* (Royal Exchange). **Television:** *Under the Sun, Henry IV, The Wimbledon Poisoner, Stalagluft.* **Film:** *Eisenstein, Shakespeare in Love, Onegin, Plunkett and Maclean, Shadowlands, Being Human, Princess Caraboo, The Fifth Element, Dangerous Beauty.*

Kostas Philippoglou
Born in Greece. He began his training at the Drama School of Athens and later continued with actor-teachers from Peter Brook's company including Tapa Sudana. He has performed in many shows in Athens, including *'Tis Pity She's a Whore* and *Sweeney Todd.* He organises workshops in Greece working with teachers from all over Europe.

Catherine Schaub Abkarian
Studied at Beaux-Arts in Bourges, France before studying Kathakali (dance-theatre from South India) for five years in France and India. She worked with Bread and Puppet Theatre and later with Théâtre du Soleil (dir. Ariane Mnouchkine) for seven years where she choreographed and performed in the chorus for *Les Atrides.* **For Complicite:** *In the Dark* (BAC). **Theatre:** *Macbeth, A Midsummer Night's Dream* (dir. Paul Golub); *Ecoute Ailleurs!* (promenades

musicales with musician Jean-Jacques Lemetre); *L'Orestie* (dir. Sylviu Purcanete); *Love's Labours Lost, L'Ultime Chant de Troie* (dir. Simon Abkarian); *Sapho de Mythilene* (dir. Agnes Delume).

Christopher Shutt
Trained at Bristol Old Vic Theatre School. He was Head of Sound at the Bristol Old Vic and the Royal Court Theatre where shows include *Serious Money* and *Road.* **For Complicite:** *The Noise of Time, The Caucasian Chalk Circle, The Street of Crocodiles, The Three Lives of Lucie Cabrol.* **For the RNT:** *Life x Three, Machinal, The Homecoming, Death of a Salesman, Chips with Everything, Not About Nightingales, Haroun and the Sea of Stories, Sleep With Me, The Darker Face of the Earth, Albert Speer, Hamlet, In Extremis/De Profundis.* Chris was awarded the 1999 New York Drama Desk Award for Outstanding Sound Design for *Not About Nightingales* on Broadway. He is currently Sound Supervisor at the RNT.

Daniel Wahl
Born in Switzerland. Trained at the Drama Academy in Zürich. Daniel is an actor, writer and director. **Theatre:** *Leone and Lena, Zettels Traum, Ahimsha, Sweet Hamlet, TodlicheStille unter dem Eis.* Worked for Pro

Helvetica Cairo and toured his own play *Desert Sand and Meilting Snow*. Wrote and directed *Captain Handicap*. Daniel has worked extensively in Switerland, Germany, Austria, Egypt, Riga and New York.

Rod Wilson
Trained in Music at Exeter University. **For Complicite:** *Light*. **Other Theatre:** Polka Theatre and Grange Park Opera 2000. **TV:** *Kid in the Corner, Snap, Mike and Angelo*. **Film:** *The Wedding Tackle, The Last Minute, I Want You, Resurrection Man*.

Mnemonic

Complicite

Note

From Scene Three onwards the Company remain on the stage throughout the performance. As the actors are already on stage, many of the characters' entrances and exits are not signalled in the stage directions.

The cuts between the scenes are fast and fluid.

Scene One

Front cloth. An empty stage except for a chair and a stone DSC.

Simon   Good evening, ladies and gentlemen. Before we start the show I'd like to say one or two words about memory. Yesterday somebody asked me why are you doing a show about memory and I was trying to remember . . . the origin of this show which is as much about origins as it is about memory.

Perhaps it is because one of the last great mysteries is the one we carry inside our heads. How we remember, why we remember, what we remember.

Or perhaps the reason is a little more prosaic . . . maybe it is simply that they say that the human memory starts to degenerate when you are only twenty-eight years old and as I am now over forty the matter is becoming a little pressing.

People used to believe that individual memories were stored and carried in individual brain cells. To retrieve a memory, therefore, all the brain had to do was to identify the relevant brain cell, get into it and . . . wham . . . there was the memory. Like an image on a hard disk in a computer. Call up the relevant folder on your desktop, double-click, double-click on file and . . . wham . . . image appears. Exactly the same each time. My God, how wonderful that would be . . . exactly the same each time. No variation. Of course we know it's not true because we know that when we remember it comes out slightly . . . different each time.

Modern theories of memory revolve around the idea of fragmentation. Different elements are, apparently, stored in different areas of the brain. And it is not so much the cells that are important in the act of memory, but the connections between the cells, the synapses, the synaptic connections. And these connections are being made and remade. Constantly. Even as I am talking to you part of your brain is changing. You are literally developing new connections between the neurons. They are being fabricated

even as I speak. It's a process called sprouting. Think of
that; you are all madly sprouting as I stand here, the
biochemical ferment going on between the cells is
unimaginable. And with the thousands of these connections
being sprouted as I speak, we can think of memory as a
pattern, a map. But not a stable neatly printed ordnance-
survey map, but one that is constantly changing and
developing. Each time we read the map, thousands of roads
have been added and all the contours have shifted; so the
action of memory therefore is kind of demented and
unimaginably high-speed orienteering round the landscape
of the brain . . . so perhaps what happens as we get older is
that we lose our compass? It's constantly changing. We
don't have any idea of why, when or how it is going to
change we only know that it will. It's like the weather;
completely unpredictable. Anyway, our job, the job of
remembering is to *reassemble*, to literally re-member, put the
relevant members back together. But what I am getting at is
that re-membering is essentially not only an act of retrieval
but a creative thing, it happens in the moment, it's an act,
an act . . . of the imagination.

Of course if memory *is* this chaotic map its highly likely that
you will lose your way and retrieve or imagine something
you didn't expect because you take a different route than
the one you thought you should . . . for example, as I stand
here trying to remember my text, for some reason my father
is coming in to my mind. Why is that? Probably it's to do
with this thing about origins, because he was an
archaeologist and so was fascinated by origins . . . he died
twenty years ago, actually, and he was American, if we are
talking about origins, and my mother is Irish, well, part
Irish, part Scottish, part Welsh, part English, which I
suppose makes me British, and that reminds me that on the
way to the theatre tonight I was in a minicab with a driver
who had a very strong accent, so I asked him where he was
from and he said 'Islington', so I said, 'No, I mean before
that, originally,' and he said, 'Well, I used to work in

Germany,' so I said, 'You don't have a German accent,' and he said, 'I'm not, I'm Greek.'

And there you are . . . I started off with brain cells and now here I am in Greece. Talking of which, the word *hippocampus* is the Greek for seahorse. That would be irrelevant were it not for the fact that it is the name of the gland which helps us to choose what we remember. Hippocampus. We need to choose what we remember because if we were to remember everything then . . . And the hippocampus is a chilli-pepper-sized, gland, well, seahorse-sized, actually, situated here at the base of brain. And the way it chooses is to fasten upon either something we already know or what we have an emotional attachment to. So, for example, perhaps I thought about my father because this chair was his. I *know* it. He sat on it. And so did my grandfather. In fact, it's a chair I know very well because I have used it in several of my shows. It was in a show called *The Chairs*, actually . . . but there we go, I'm rerouting already, quick, back on to the right track . . . also the hippocampus locks on to what we emotionally relate to, so that, for example, if I was in love, to look at this floor would remind me of my lover: Oh God, she walked here, or this rock, here she tripped so beautifully, or this chair, this is where she sat, her back, her arms, her arse . . . sorry . . . but you, for example, are unlikely to remember that I have a blue shirt as opposed to a yellow one unless I attach it to something, for example, if I go *Whoo* you will get a slight fright and therefore remember the colour of my shirt. *Whoo . . . Whoo . . .* you see . . . *Whoo* gives you a shock, which sets off a series of electrical reactions which will tell the brain to sprout more connections and you will remember . . . or perhaps you will remember because it is so strange to see the director standing up in front of the audience going whoo, whoo, whoo.

Yes, mnemonics are frequently useless objects which are there for no other reason than to help us remember. For example, we carry a wedding ring to remind us that we are married, or a watch to remind us of the time. Useless objects. And I am carrying this rock in my pocket to remind me not to go on for too long. And a second rock to remind me to take another rock out of this pocket which is there to remind me to tell you to turn off your mobile phones. If anybody's mobile phone goes off during the performance they will be forcibly ejected from the auditorium and a letter will be written to their parents. There's a woman halfway up this aisle here, a woman with blonde hair, who's frantically reaching into her bag. So if everybody looks at her she'll start feeling extremely embarrassed and she'll squirt from her hippocampus and start sprouting madly and she'll never forget to turn off her mobile phone again.

And now, ladies and gentlemen, all of this is leading to ask you to remember that when you came in on the back of your chair you had a little plastic bag. Pick it up, please. Open it and take out the contents. In it you will find a leaf and a sleeping blind such as you would find on transatlantic flights . . . the blind not the leaf, I mean. And I know what you are thinking, you're thinking, oh my God, audience participation. But it's all right. I am not going to spit chewed banana at you or rub my body in baby oil and then squirm all over the front row, no, 1968 is a long time ago . . . more's the pity. No, I want you simply to put the blind on . . . your head and hold the leaf in your hand. Because before we offer you some of our fragments, we would like you to reassemble some fragments of your own. Now, ladies and gentlemen, we would like you to think back, to remember.

Blackout.

Think back to a time which is not very long ago. Last Sunday morning. You wake up. Where are you? What is the weather like? Who do you see? How do you feel? The memory of last Sunday probably comes back very quickly so now we go even further back. New Year's Day 1999. You wake up. Where are you? Do you have a hangover? What do you feel? Who do you see? Look out of the window . . . What is the weather like? Can you remember what you think? Perhaps you can remember a little but not everything

of that day. A few fragments. So now we will go further
back. To autumn 1991. September. Where are you? Can
you remember? It's just after the Gulf War and before
Yugoslavia starts to split apart. Perhaps it's completely
empty in your imagination. Perhaps it rushes back because
of a particular event. Or perhaps there are one or two
fragments . . .

But now we will go even further back. We will go to when
you are six years old. It's summer. Or perhaps your first day
at school, or pre-school, primary school. Look down at your
feet. What shoes are you wearing? Look behind you, to the
right, hold up your hand in your imagination. Another hand
clasps yours. It is your mother. Look up to your left.
Another hand clasps that one. It is your father. Your
mother, your father and you. And now look back behind
your right-hand side. Behind your mother, with a hand on
each of her shoulders, are her parents. Her mother and her
father. Your grandparents. And to the left, on your father's
shoulder, are his parents. His mother. His father. Six people
stand behind you. All looking at you. And now look back
again and behind your grandparents are their parents. Eight
great-grandparents, four grandparents, your parents and
you. And behind the eight of them are sixteen others all
looking at you. Now feel the leaf. It has several veins.
Imagine that each vein is a line of your ancestry all coming
down to you, the stalk. All of them leading to you. In one
hundred years there are four generations. If you look back
along the line behind you, as you look back, at the
beginning of the nineteenth century standing in that line of
ancestors are 256 of your relatives. At the beginning of the
eighteenth century, assuming there are no kinship ties, there
is a line of 4,064. At the beginning of the seventeenth
century there are 64,000 and in the sixteenth 1.5 million.
And a thousand years ago, if there really were no kinship
ties, that line would be longer than all people who have ever
been born. Which, of course, is not possible . . . but it means
that you are related to everyone sitting in this theatre.

Lights up to reveal **Simon** *on stage. Changed into the character* **Virgil** *who is listening to the voice of the man, the director who introduced the show. The audience should have been completely unaware of when the change between live and recorded voice took place.* **Virgil** *has a mask and is holding a leaf.*

Simon (*VO*)   And now, ladies and gentlemen, gently, very gently so that the light doesn't affect your eyes, take off your blindfold. Now look at the leaf that you have in your hands. (*Pause.*) Turn it over and look at the veins. From the stalk there are five other stalks. Look at the lines of your ancestry, the patterns on it. Imagine that they are each a line of your ancestry. And there are other stalks coming from it. If you look closer still, there are even more stalks, interlocking, and tinier veins, branching and branching and branching, making more and more patterns (*SFX – A mobile phone starts to ring*) . . . in an infinite variety of ways, interconnections but repeating patterns . . .

Virgil *eventually realizes that it is his phone. He answers. The other voice continues.*

Virgil   Hello. Who is this? Who? . . . Alice? Oh my God. I'm in the theatre. Don't go away. I'll go out. Hang on, for God's sake, don't go away.

He makes his way out of the theatre.

Simon (*VO*)   . . . all the same patterns. A repeating pattern . . . a self-similar pattern.

Virgil   Listen, I'm on my way out, hang on . . . (*to imaginary audience*) sorry . . . sorry . . .

Simon (*VO*)   The same pattern that is in this leaf is in your blood system which goes from your arteries to your veins, to your capillaries until the capillaries are no more than a cell wide.

Virgil   I'm only whispering because it's still going on . . .

Simon (*VO*)   If you take a photograph of the delta of a river, from space, you find the same pattern.

Virgil I'm in the foyer now . . . Alice?

Man (*at the other end of the phone*) I'm sorry?

Virgil What? Hello, Alice?

Man What? Hello?

Virgil Oh, Jesus, it's you. You sounded like a woman.

Man It's me, Alex.

Virgil Yes, you sounded like Alice.

Man Really?

Virgil Oh God . . . I was miles away.

Man Where are you?

Virgil Well, I was in a theatre, in the middle of a show . . .

Man You were in the theatre? What were you doing in the theatre, for God's sake?

Virgil I don't know. Why does anyone go to the theatre?

Man I'll call you later. Go back in.

Virgil No, no, I can't, it's much too embarrassing . . .

Man What were you seeing?

Virgil . . . listen, it's very strange. I thought I was going to see some dance, or something . . . it's this company that people said were really physical, apparently they used to be funny . . .

Man Yes?

Virgil But what in fact happened was that this guy came on and started to talk about memory.

Man . . . a lecture?

Virgil No, no . . . we all got these plastic bags and we had to put on these blindfolds, I've still got mine on, actually, like you get on aeroplanes and we were clutching these leaves and all sitting there in the dark imagining our ancestors, like some kind of mass seance, the entire audience . . .

Man   Strange . . .

Virgil   Yes, really peculiar. It made me feel very strange and then he said look down at your feet when you're five years old and think what shoes you're wearing and I saw those kind of Clarks' sandals . . .

Man   Start-Rite?

Virgil   Yes, Start-Rite. But it was so strange. It set off this terrible train of thoughts for me. Listen, have you got a moment?

Man   Yes, come over.

Virgil   No, no. I just want to explain what happened, why I should think it was Alice's voice. Where are you?

Man   I'm in the garden.

Virgil   You're in your garden? Right, well, get hold of a leaf.

Man   OK.

Virgil   Have you got one?

Man   Yes.

Virgil   Right, now shut your eyes.

Man   Uh-uh.

Virgil   Now imagine that you are five years old. Reach up your left hand. Another hand takes hold of yours. It's your mother. And behind you on the right is your father. Your mother, your father and you. Now behind them are your grandparents.

Man   Yes.

Virgil   There's four of them.

Man   Yes.

Virgil   And behind them are your great-grandparents.
Eight of them. And behind your great-grandparents are
your great-great-grandparents. There are sixteen of them.

Virgil *turns to the audience. He is no longer talking on the phone. He
is listening. As if he is remembering it. This effect is achieved once
again by making an invisible join between the live telephone
conversation and the recording.* **Virgil** *picks up the chair from DSC
and switches on the TV. In its glow, he holds up the leaf as if recalling
the conversation.*

Man (*VO*)   Yes.

Virgil (*VO*)   So it makes a pattern coming down to you.

Man (*VO*)   It's beautiful.

Virgil (*VO*)   Right, now feel the leaf.

Man (*VO*)   Yes.

Virgil (*VO*)   Now the pattern on the leaf is chaotic.

Man (*VO*)   It's very rough.

Virgil (*VO*)   This is what he's getting at. The further back
we go, the more chaotic our interrelationships become. In
other words we do not know where we come from.

Virgil *suddenly starts to think about this again. He pulls out his
mobile.*

Man (*VO*)   Explain it to me again, I'm a bit lost.

Virgil (*VO*)   This pattern of our ancestry. This genetic
pattern is the same as the pattern on the leaf. Do you get it?

Man (*VO*)   Yes.

Virgil (*VO*)   In other words, it's fractal.

Virgil *dials. We hear the phone ringing at the other end.*

Man (*VO*)   So the pattern on the leaf is a description of our
ancestry?

Virgil (*VO*)   That's right, yes. Our ancestry is actually chaotic and interlinked just like the veins on a leaf.

Man (*VO*)   It's bizarre.

Virgil (*VO*)   In other words we don't know where we begin. We know that we're here but we don't know why.

The phone is answered and the first conversation continues in the background, as this new one starts.

Man   226 7204

Virgil   It's me again.

Man   Hello.

Virgil   I've just been thinking about what we were talking about earlier.

Man   Well, listen, could you remember it tomorrow? I'm just going to bed, actually.

Virgil   What's the time?

Man   It's eleven.

Virgil   God, you go to bed early.

Man   Well, some of us have kids.

Virgil   I just wanted to explain it another way. I was just thinking, why did you phone me?

Man   To ask if you wanted me to come round with the van and help you move out.

Virgil   There's practically nothing here. But why did you phone me? What made you think of me?

Man   Well, I was sorting out some stuff and I saw an old picture of you and Alice.

Virgil   You found a picture of Alice at the moment I was starting to think about her, I guarantee it. So you see the connection?

Man   What, synchronicity?

Virgil   No, it's nothing to do with synchronicity. Let me explain it another way. For example, why have I just lost my job?

Man   Well, they were going to get you sooner or later.

Virgil   No, no, why did I take that job in the first place?

Man   It's a mystery.

Virgil   I'll tell you exactly why. It all came flooding back to me. I suddenly had this image. What happened was that it was pissing with rain, it poured for about three hours, so I went out later than usual. By the time I got to the newsagent's they'd sold out of all newspapers. So for some inexplicable reason I picked up a copy of *Geology Today*.

Man   So, it's all the fault of the weather?

Virgil   No.

Man   If you're looking for one event which is going to explain why everything happened and why you're in such a mess, you're not going to find it.

Virgil   No, no, I'm not, I'm saying the opposite . . . it's all out of control, it's chaos and we don't know why or how chaos occurs but there is a pattern to it, this pattern is completely unpredictable. It's a question of how we live with that unpredictability.

Virgil's *chair collapses.*

Virgil   Fucking hell.

Man   Hello, hello.

Virgil   My fucking chair's just collapsed. It really hurt.

Man   Your chair's just collapsed? Where are you?

Virgil   Well . . . I'm at home.

Virgil *turns slowly on himself, mirroring the turning of his thoughts, as his room – table, bed and sink – assembles around him. A plastic curtain creates a wall. He ends up sitting on his bed looking at the television.*

Broadcast *(VO)*   Early in 1938 engineers of the American electronics company Westinghouse Electrics decided that the technology had arrived that would enable them to create a time capsule capable of lasting 5,000 years, a period which roughly equates with recorded history. They believed that they could overcome the major problems that arise in such a project: how to construct a vessel that would not perish, how to make sure it would be found so far in the future and what to put in it that would be truly representative of our civilization. They decided that . . .

Scene Two

Inside **Virgil***'s room.* **Virgil** *stands looking out of his window DSC and dials.*

Virgil   Hello.

Man   Hello.

Virgil   Hi, it's me again.

Man   Oh God.

Virgil   I was just thinking about Alice.

Man   Have you any idea what time it is?

Virgil   Um, no. I was thinking about why she left.

Man   It's two thirty in the morning.

Virgil   Well, never mind, I was awake anyway. The point being, you know, why did she leave?

Man   I'm just going out of the bedroom.

Virgil   Yes, but she left eight months ago.

Man I'm sorry . . . I . . .

Virgil She didn't say why. All she left was this answerphone message. Did I ever play it to you? No? Well, listen to this. Let me play it to you.

The message plays.

Alice (*VO*) You have to wait now and this time you follow me.

Virgil Can you hear the inherent contradiction in that? You have to wait and follow. It's impossible. And I suddenly realized what's happening to her . . . What's going on is that she's feeding back on herself. It's feedback, turbulence. Her internal state is like the weather. Our internal lives are a mystery. We don't even really know what causes us to sleep. My doctor can tell me I've got insomnia but he doesn't know how or why.

Man I don't have insomnia.

Virgil Yes, yes, but the point is that Alice is in a state of turbulence.

Man Go to bed.

Virgil And what is turbulence?

Man Go to bed.

Virgil Look, turbulence is fluid motion become random. Our emotions are essentially fluid.

Man Just fuck off.

Virgil We have the . . . hello . . . hello, oh shit.

Alice (*VO*) You have to wait now and this time you follow me.

He turns on answer machine and listens to the message from **Alice** *over and over. 'You have to wait now and this time you follow me.' He plunges his head into water. Darkness. White noise of mobiles going crazy. Loud music. Lies on bed. Tries a position to go to sleep. Blackout.*

SFX – **Alice***'s voice continues. Tries another position on the bed.*
Blackout. SFX – **Alice***'s voice continues. Tries another position on the*
floor against the bed. Blackout. SFX – **Alice***'s voice continues. Tries*
another position on the table. Blackout. SFX – **Alice***'s voice continues.*
Tries another position on the floor against the chair. Blackout. SFX –
Alice*'s voice continues. Tries another position DSC floor. Blackout.*
SFX – **Alice***'s voice continues. Tries another position back on the bed.*

Alice *(VO)*   I can't tell you where I'm going, I just have to
go.

SFX transposes into loud wind, voices. **Virgil** *takes his pillow and*
lies on the stone.

Scene Three

The wind increases. The company move on, slowly. They cross the
stage. The plastic curtain is drawn slowly back.

Virgil *(VO)*   Who can say what caused a high-level
southerly air current between the fifth and eighth of March
1991 to transport a Saharan dust which darkened the sky
and fell over a wide area of the Austrian Alps colouring the
snow and the fields a yellowish brown? It could have been
the movement of a camel, a mountaineer's sweat, a man
riding a bicycle. All movements of the earth contribute to
the chaotic movement of the weather.

They move in the wind.

Virgil *(VO)*   The Saharan dust meant that sunlight was no
longer reflected by white snow fields. Instead, the dark
yellow layer of dust absorbed the radiation and accelerated
the disappearance of snow on the melting glacier.

The others sit and we see the **Simons***. They are dressed in*
mountaineering clothing, standing on the bed and table as if on the
mountain top.

Helmut *(VO)*   From a distance of eight to ten metres, we
saw something sticking out of the ice. Our first thought was

that it was rubbish, perhaps even a doll, because there is plenty of litter, even in the high mountains. But as we came closer Erika said, 'But it's a man.'

They make their way to the body and stand still. A camera flashes.

Erika *(VO)*   Ja, we thought it was a mountaineer who'd died there. We were shocked. We didn't touch the body. There was just a blue ski clip lying nearby and Helmut took a photograph as a record.

Helmut *(VO)*   There was an injury on the head and it looked like the arms were missing.

Scene Four

SFX – Train. The Eurostar train. **Alice** *sits as though looking out of the train window.* **Virgil** *sits up violently as if woken from a dream. He's looking at* **Alice** *as if what he sees he is imagining or remembering.*

Telephone *(VO)*   Message received today at three forty-three p.m.

Virgil *(VO)*   Hi, Alice, it's me. Listen, you go to your mother's funeral and you leave me a message telling me I have to wait months before you come back. OK, you telephone but what am I supposed to do with a telephone?

Telephone *(VO)*   To erase the message press two. Message erased. Message received fourteen December 1998.

Virgil *(VO)*   Hi. Call me. Bye.

Telephone *(VO)*   Message erased.

Alice *(VO)*   You have to wait now and this time you follow me.

Virgil *turns slowly while a phone rings and the next scene begins. He is caught between worlds. It is the police station where they are registering the find of the body.*

Scene 5

SFX – Phone. **Koler** *answers it.*

Koler   Polizei Imst, Koler . . . Was? Nein, I hob jetzt koa Zeit . . . Ruf mi später wieder an, ge, ja? Servus.

Puts down phone.

Koler   Peter, was hammer g'schrieben?

Peter   Alpine incident: body discovered at Hauslabjoch.

Koler   Climbers descending the Finailspitze discovered a body sticking out of the ice. Identity not yet established. Judging by the equipment this was an Alpine accident going back many years, perhaps as long ago as the Second World War. In 1941 a mountaineer walking the exact same route went missing and is still unaccounted for.

Virgil *moves back to the bed watching while* **Capsoni** *replaces him lying on the rock.*

Capsoni   Carlo Capsoni was born on the eleventh of March 1903 in Piacenza.

We hear a Bach fugue. **Capsoni** *climbs upwards, as though on the mountainside, and takes his place at the piano.*

The son of Giovanni and Maraya Capsoni, he was a music professor, a lover of the pianoforte and an experienced mountaineer . . . .

The fugue ends and a student, **Salvatore***, enters.*

Capsoni   There, you see, it's just a matter of technique and some imagination. Now come in. Don't be frightened, as you were last week. It's a piano not a rattlesnake.

He gestures to the table which **Salvatore** *sits down at as if it were a piano.* **Capsoni** *looks out of the window DS.*

Capsoni   A strange mist on the Finailspitze but they say that it will clear up later.

He gestures at a piece of music.

From the beginning. Right hand only.

The student begins the fugue but his fear means that he tortures the music. **Capsoni** *punctuates the music with cries of 'No, no!'*

Yes, well, we have a mountain to climb, you and I.

He becomes increasingly frustrated.

Salvatore, Salvatore. You can play this piece of music, I've heard you do it. When we play a piece of music for another person we often feel frightened, sick with fear, like a mountaineer with vertigo.

His tone softens.

Why? Because we feel naked. And what does nakedness remind us of? It reminds us that our fears are natural, that we are all vulnerable. So, let us agree that we are both frightened, stark naked and that we climb this mountain together. So from the beginning. Right hand only. With fear. And once you start you must not look down.

The student begins to play. This time the fear is vanishing.

Capsoni   That's it. Yes, yes, the mist is clearing. Now, both hands. Allegro. Yes, yes. Up, up, up the Finailspitze.

The student is playing marvellously.

Capsoni   On the twenty-fifth of August 1941, Carlo Capsoni ascended the Hochjoch, having left word that he intended to walk on his own to the Similaunhütte via the Schöne Aussicht. He was never seen again.

Scene Six

Virgil *mirrors the actions of* **Capsoni** *as he remembers climbing the mountain and then collapses back on to the stone as SFX – Eurostar train.*

Koler (*VO*)   A music professor by name of Capsoni is still missing, still missing.

Alice *listens to her phone.*

Telephone   Message received fourteen December 1998.

Virgil (*VO*)   Alice, me again. Listen, what's going on?

Telephone   Message erased.

Scene Seven

SFX – Wind. The wind is ear-splitting.

Virgil (*VO*)   Friday, the twentieth of September 1991.

SFX – Helicopter. Two mountaineers signal to a helicopter.

SFX – Loud drill noises. They turn and approach the body.

Koler (*VO*)   Sticking out of the ice was the sunburnt head, neck and shoulders of a man. On his back I saw black lines. I thought maybe they were burn marks.

They begin to use a pneumatic chisel to get the body out of the ice.

Koler (*VO*)   He was not like other glacier corpses, this one didn't give off a smell.

They chisel some more.

Koler (*VO*)   The skin was just like leather.

Pirpamer *helps* **Koler** *to try and lift the body.*

Koler (*VO*)   We tried with the pneumatic chisel but it kept on slipping. Unfortunately a couple of times it went right into his left thigh.

They cover the body with a plastic sheet.

Koler (*VO*)   No we couldn't free him. It got so bad, the weather, we tried and tried but we couldn't get the body out.

Scene Eight

SFX – Eurostar train, **Alice** *travelling.*

Train (*VO*)   Ladies and gentlemen, in a few minutes we will be entering the Channel Tunnel; the crossing will take approximately twenty minutes. Mesdames et messieurs, ans quelques instants nous entrons dans le tunnel sous la manche. Cette traversée va durer vingt minutes. Merci.

Scene Nine

SFX – Wind. A lone climber arrives to look at the body. He is an immigrant, a trainee cook.

Virgil (*VO*)   Saturday, twenty-first of September 1991.

Cook (*VO*)   I am from Slovenia. I am working in the local hotel. When I was told about the body I decided to see for myself. About twenty or thirty people have already been to look. They said he was a soldier from the beginning of the century. I had to go up twice because the first time for me the sight of the plastic bag was enough, but then I couldn't get him out of my mind.

He looks under the plastic. Shocked, he stands back.

Yes, there really is a dead man under there.

Scene Ten

SFX – Eurostar, **Alice** *travelling.*

Train (*VO*)   Mesdames et messieurs, bienvenue en France. Il est maintenant dix-sept heure dix, heure locale. Ladies and gentlemen, welcome to France. If you wish to set your watches, the time is now five ten p.m.

Alice *picks up the phone.*

Telephone   Message received fourteen December 1998.

Virgil (*VO*)   Hi, it's me.

He sits up again remembering his own message to her.

Virgil (*VO*)   Listen, I quite understand that you didn't want me to come to your mother's funeral but it just would have been nice to see you before you left. Where are you, by the way?

Again she cuts him off.

Telephone   Message erased.

She looks out of the window. The vision fades as **Virgil** *stands up and puts his foot on the rock DSC.*

Scene Eleven

The standing on the rock stimulates **Virgil**'s *memory.*

Alice (*VO*)   Read it to me again.

Virgil (*VO*)   Why.

Alice (*VO*)   Just read it.

Virgil (*VO*)   OK. (*Reads.*) Nature has arranged matters so that the bio-mass of every living creature is after death reintegrated into the natural cycle by way of a very variable food chain.

He goes to the sink to try and wash away the voices, but they still continue.

Virgil (*VO*)   Only man upset this sensible rule when he began to reflect on life after death, resulting in burials that sometimes raise the dead into the sky as in the towers of silence in Persia on whose platforms the dead are offered to the vultures.

He moves back to the rock; behind him are two shadowy figures.

Virgil (*VO*)   Sometimes burning them. Sometimes burying them in the ground. Sometimes preserving them for the life to come.

Virgil *moves back, revealing* **Simonides** *and his mother standing before the rock as if it is a grave. He sits on his bed listening to the scene as if he has heard it before. The space opens out as the light of an Athenian evening fills the stage.* **Simonides** *kisses his father's headstone and lights a cigarette. His mother crosses herself.*

Simonides   Hello, Father, how are you? You looked so beautiful when we buried you here in your new suit.

He breaks the cigarette in half and puts one half on the gravestone.

This will be your last cigarette, Father. I'm afraid you have to give up smoking. I'm leaving. I'm leaving Greece. There is no future for me here. I have to find it somewhere else. I was going to Germany to work for BMW. I passed the medical examination, everything, but in the end they didn't want me. You know why? Because of you, Father. Because you fought as a partisan in the Second World War, you communist. For me you were always the mountain, for them you're just a communist. You have made me politically undesirable.

But, anyway, I found a solution. I bought a first-class ticket to Germany. I will travel first class. Nobody questions a rich man. The ticket was very very expensive. I had to sell the house, Father, I don't need it any more. Don't worry about Mama. She will stay with Maria. Yia sou patera.

Mother   Μη φύγεις παιδι μου. Μη φύγεις
          Mi phygis pedi mou. Mi phygis.

Simonides   Δε γίεταί μάνα, πρέπει. Είναι για το
          καλό μου, για το μέλλον μον
          De ginete mana, prepi. Ine gia to kalo mou,
          gia to melon mou.

Mother   Να ξανάρθεις
          Na xanarthis.

Simonides   Κα λά, θα δούμε. Να ιου πούμε το
τραγούδι του;
Kala, tha dourne. Na tou pourne to tragoudi
tou?

Mother   Ναι.
Ne.

They start to sing a rembatica, mournful. **Virgil** *returns to the rock as
they retreat upstage. The room returns around him and he continues
thinking about the previous conversation.*

Alice *(VO)*   I don't know.

Virgil *(VO)*   What?

Alice *(VO)*   What my mother would have wanted. I think
I'd have preferred to offer my body to the vultures. Read
some more.

Virgil *(VO)*   It's a bit morbid.

Alice *(VO)*   I know, but I like it.

Virgil *(VO)*   OK. The practice of giving a human being a
dignified funeral is so firmly rooted in the culture of most
societies as to be hardly without exception.

Virgil *lies down on the rock again.*

Scene Twelve

*Cross-fade to the mountain top. SFX – Helicopter. A terrible wind.
The whole company stand and gaze at* **Virgil**'s *body, he has become
the Iceman.*

Virgil *(VO)*   Monday, twenty-third of September 1991: the
day of the official recovery.

One of the rescuers gazes out at the audience, the voice is clearly his.

Koler *(VO)*   I was with forensic expert Rainer Henn. We
flew up to the Hauslabjoch to finally recover the body.

(*Pause.*) It was so cold. (*Pause.*) We had no tools. We were told the body was ready but overnight the body had once more frozen into the ice.

*He organizes the attempt to get the body out of the ice, but it is a struggle. Using stones they try to chip it free. Eventually they manage it and lift **Virgil**'s body, held stiff as though frozen solid, and gently deposit it USC.*

Koler (*VO*)   Finally we got the body out of the ice. It was a shocking sight.

They stand back.

Koler (*VO*)   We didn't do up the zip because by now the body was beginning to smell.

He stands alone in a spotlight. The mountain fades.

Koler (*VO*)   They have criticized me a lot for the way the recovery was handled. These people have never been on a mountain at 3,200 metres under these conditions. It's very easy to sit in a centrally heated office.

He lifts the body together with an assistant and positions it on the table, US. The light of a forensic laboratory begins to seep on stage.

Scene Thirteen

News Broadcast   During their descent from the Finailspitze on Thursday tourists discovered a body partially emerging from the glacier below the Hauslabjoch. Only its head and shoulders were clear of the ice.

The radio report begins to fade out over the next telephone call.

News Broadcast   The warden of the refuge reported the find to the police at Sölden. Judging by the dead man's equipment, he was a mountaineer. It seems that the accident occurred some decades ago. The body has not yet been identified.

DSL there is a single spotlight on **Professor Spindler**. *He became the principal archaeologist, overseeing the entire project of the analysis of the find of the Iceman.*

Henn (*VO*)   Professor Spindler. Hello. Good morning. It's Doctor Henn from the Institute of Forensic Medicine. Would you like to see an untypical glacier corpse?

Spindler (*VO*)   Archaeologists, as a rule, do not normally associate themselves with bodies found in the ice, they are far too recent. But time and again I am moved by such a cold and lonely death. As if nature was scoffing at a puny human, depriving him of a normal burial.

Henn (*VO*)   I don't think it's recent. It looks like a very unusual case. The police thought it was a music professor who died in 1941. Other people have speculated that it is from the nineteenth century or even the Middle Ages. But, Professor, there is an object I would like you to see. It is a strange ice axe. It makes me think that it could be even earlier.

The light of the forensic laboratory fills the stage. The scientists examine the body. **Spindler** *is greeted by* **Professor Henn** *and inspects the body.*

Spindler (*VO*)   In front of me is the shrivelled corpse of a man. Naked except for a strange grass-filled shoe. Carlo Capsoni is definitely out of the running.

Spindler   My guess is that he is approximately 4,000 years old . . .

The forensic scientists all speak at once, incredulous.

Spindler   . . . and, if the dating is revised, it could be even earlier.

Virgil *sits up and moves off the table. He reaches under the bed and takes out the fragments of the chair, broken at the top of the show. These suggest the body of the Iceman.*

Virgil (*VO*)   So the man emerging out of the glacier was as a direct result of a sandstorm in North Africa.

Scene Fourteen

The reverie is broken by the flash of photographers' bulbs. The forensic scientists have become **Journalists** *who stand around* **Spindler** *throwing questions at him, as if he were at the other end of a conference chamber, all shouting at once.* **Virgil** *holds the broken chair.*

All   Can we see the body, Professor, can we see it?

Journalist 3   Why is the body naked?

Journalist 2   Was he murdered?

Journalist 1   I hear it hasn't got a dick.

Journalist 5   Is it a woman?

Spindler   Please, please, I'm not used to all these questions, one at a time please.

SFX – Music. **Virgil** *places the body on the table.* **Journalists** *again.*

Journalist 1   Herr Professor, how do we know the body is 4,000 years old?

Spindler   Carbon dating which has now put the date back another thousand years.

Journalist 4   Exactly how long?

Spindler   Think of the time between us and Socrates, then double it.

Journalist 3   Yes, but how long is that, Jesus?

Spindler   Well, it's 3,200 years before him.

Journalist 3   Who?

Spindler   Jesus.

Journalist 3   Very funny, Professor. When did he die?

Spindler   He died, as I said, 5,200 years ago.

Virgil *has picked up a pebble. Holding it stimulates his memory and the voices invade again. The presence of* **Alice** *is reinforced with a spotlight on her on the other side of the stage, fingering a stone which hangs on a string around her neck.*

Alice (*VO*)   Is it for me?

Virgil (*VO*)   Do you like it?

Alice (*VO*)   What is it?

Virgil (*VO*)   It's a rock.

Alice (*VO*)   A rock? What's it for?

Virgil (*VO*)   You wear it around your neck.

Alice (*VO*)   Why?

Virgil (*VO*)   Well, read the thing.

Alice (*VO*)   You read it.

Virgil (*VO*)   OK. Perhaps one of the most astonishing discoveries of modern times is the immensity of the past.

Journalists *again.*

Journalist 4   Who was he?

Journalist 3   Where did he come from?

Spindler   Well, we are hoping that our investigation will reveal a considerably greater understanding of . . .

Journalist 5   What did he have with him?

Spindler   A broken stick, splinters of wood . . . Scraps of leather . . . Strips of hide . . . fragments.

SFX – Music.

Virgil (*VO*)   This stone is called palaganite. It was thrown up on to the Canadian land mass twenty million years ago but it is much older than that. It is from the beginning. Palaganite is thought to be 400 million years old.

Journalists *again. They start to move downstage and* **Spindler** *is left alone.*

Journalist 5   So what is so special about this body?

Spindler   The fact that he stepped to us directly out of his everyday life, which makes him one of the most valuable finds of the century.

Journalist 3   Right, so how much is he worth, then?

Spindler   I mean to say that this body is unique. His monetary value is irrelevant. In any case it is impossible to calculate.

Journalist 5   If it is so valuable who does he belong to?

Spindler   That has yet to be determined.

SFX – Music.

Alice *(VO)*   So that's the point, is it?

Virgil *(VO)*   Yes, what you have around your neck is . . .

Alice *(VO)*   . . . 400 million years old. Mmm.

Journalists *again.*

Journalist 1   Herr Professor, apparently he was found on the frontier?

Spindler   Yes.

Journalist 3   Which frontier?

Spindler   On the frontier between north and south Tyrol.

Journalist 3   In Austria?

Spindler   No, no, on the border between Austria and Italy.

Journalist 2   So who does he belong to?

Spindler   At present, the University of Innsbruck.

Journalist 3   Which is where?

Spindler   Austria.

Journalist 4   He must have been on one or other side of the frontier so which side of the border was he lying?

Spindler   That is being looked into, we think probably . . . Italy.

An immediate clamouring response from all the **Journalists** *as they scent a story.*

Journalist 1   Herr Professor, with all due respect, before 1919 this entire area, including the place where the body was found, belonged to Austria, to be precise the Austro-Hungarian Empire. Would you care to comment?

Spindler   No.

Virgil *moves across stage, following* **Alice** *in his mind. Her face appears momentarily. He hears a train – SFX. He moves back towards the bed.*

Virgil (*VO*)   Hi. It's me. Listen, I quite understand that you didn't want me to come to your mother's funeral but it just would have been nice to see you before you left. Where are you by the way? Where are you? Where are you?

Scene Fifteen

During the following scene the Iceman is dehumanized by becoming public property, a national monument. **Alice** *appears, as if in* **Virgil***'s imagination, USL behind the two-way mirror. She is on the telephone. The debate between the* **Italians** *and the* **Austrians** *about who the body belongs to centres first around the bed, using* **Virgil***'s knee as the mountain top, then around the table which moves DSC. At the same time the forensic analysis of the Iceman's body takes place around the table.*

Italian   Italia. So contrary to the assumption of the first few days, the site of the finds may after all be on Italian territory.

Spindler   Many people think that the Iceman is such an important link with our ancient past that they should be able to view the body.

Innsbruck   Yes, yes. I see your point.

A telephone rings. An Austrian **Clerk** *answers.*

Lawyer (*on telephone*)   Good morning. I'm making a claim for the body found on the Similaun glacier on behalf of my clients, the inhabitants of the Austrian district of Sölden, because without doubt the person lived within their district.

Clerk   May I remind your client that the body is over 5,000 years old. Good day.

She slams down the phone.

Spindler   The body. Sodden body. No head hair, body hair or pubic hair.

The two representatives return to either side of the bed, still attempting to determine the exact position of the body.

Italian   Our police are presently up at 3,200 metres measuring the frontier. With rob.

Innsbruck   With rob?

Italian   Yes, rob!

Innsbruck   Rob?

He holds out a piece of rope.

Italian   Rob!

Innsbruck   Oh . . . rope, rope.

Spindler   The body lay in a gully to the side of the glacier, so in over 5,000 years the forces in the ice rotated him through only ninety degrees.

Back to the two representatives.

Innsbruck   Yes, well, our men are up there too.

Italian   I'm afraid they will have to show us their passports as they are on our territory.

A multiple image appears. **Spindler** *in the forensic lab, his face on the television screen. The police on the mountain top attempting to determine the body's location.* **Alice** *appears USL behind the two-way mirror.* **Virgil** *lifts the chair from the table. For a brief moment it appears as a body.*

Virgil (*VO*)   How many mourned him when he disappeared? He has gone to the mountain, is that what they said? How many songs did he know?

Italian   . . . tells us that the spot is on Italian territory by approximately three lengths.

Innsbruck   Three lengths?

Italian   Three lengths of rope – roughly 120 metres.

Clerk *answers the telephone.*

German Woman (*on telephone*)   Hello, hello, this is Anna Schmidt calling from Munich. I've just seen the Iceman on the television and I think he is my grandfather.

Clerk *slams down the phone.*

Spindler   Chest and abdomen sunken, in the eye sockets eyeballs are still recognizable.

Innsbruck   Yes, yes, I understand that it is three rope lengths your side of the frontier and therefore . . .

Italian   . . . he is Italian . . .

Innsbruck   Yes.

Italian   . . . from the south Tyrol, but I'd like to know what steps are being taken to protect the body . . .

Spindler   The black marks on the back of the Iceman have now been identified as tattoos. He had many of these across his body, for example, behind the right knee a tattooed cross, bluish in colour.

Clerk *answers the telephone.*

Australian (*on telephone*)   Hello, my name is Clare Mulvaney. I'm calling from Sydney, Australia. Look I'm having IVF treatment at the moment and I wondered if there's any chance of some of that Neolithic sperm coming my way.

She slams the phone down.

Spindler   Although the external organs are foliated the body is definitely male.

Italian   . . . and we are very concerned to hear that the climbers from Nuremberg, who found it first, have already filed a claim for ownership under the Austrian treasure-trove legislation.

Innsbruck   Treasure?

Italian   Treasure.

Innsbruck   I'm not sure if a corpse is treasure . . .

Italian   Which means they can claim half the find.

Innsbruck   Half the body?

Spindler   So the idea has taken shape that the naked corpse of this dead man should be put on public display. I think the question needs to be addressed of whether this is compatible with human dignity.

Italian   . . . but Austrian law does not provide for a human body to qualify as an ancient monument.

Innsbruck   Perhaps the tattooing on the body's back should be classed as a work of art. Like that it could be . . . .

The phone rings, then another, then another. A collage of calls and multiple conversations build in intensity as everyone attempts to get a piece of the Iceman. At its peak it cuts to a sudden silence.

Innsbruck (*on the telephone*)   And you can explain to them that I have been given jurisdiction by the relevant authorities to announce that, as of this moment . . .

Spindler   . . . the body is officially an ancient monument.

There is the sound of applause. A metal frame is held US of the table. The body has become a chair. The people gaze dispassionately through the window, rubbernecking the chair.

Virgil (*VO*)   Naked except for a strange grass-filled shoe.

The image is reversed. The frame is now DS. The people looking US at the Iceman. **Spindler** *lectures, holding a microphone.* **Virgil** *crouches disconsolately on the bed. He turns towards the headboard as a video is projected on to his back. This is a live projection.*

Spindler   So the skin, which is now leathery and tough, changes colour across the body. If you look through the window of the refrigeration chamber, you can see that it ranges from a pale ivory, through brown, to almost black. The chamber is kept strictly between zero and minus six degrees Celsius, and there is a degree of humidity which keeps it at the mean annual temperature of the Hauslabjoch. You can see marks on the body. These marks are tattoos. There are fifty-seven tattoos on his body.

A pen draws the Iceman's tattoos live on to the projection on **Virgil**'s *chest.*

They were there because of pain. The skin was punctured, scored or cut with a very sharp instrument. A coloured paste, most likely a combination of charcoal and saliva, was then rubbed in. They are certainly not branding or lash marks. X-rays of the bones adjacent to the tattoos show degenerative changes indicating that the Iceman was suffering from severe arthritis and rheumatism. Now if we look more closely at where the marks are concentrated on the backs of his legs and the lower lumber region of the spine we can see that he could not have done them himself. This was an ongoing course of treatment administered by someone with the ability to heal, possibly from his own community.

Scene Sixteen

Virgil'*s mobile phone rings. He turns DS to answer it. The video image is now unclear.*

Virgil   Hello.

Alice   Hello. It's me.

Long pause. **Alice**'*s face appears gradually on* **Virgil**'*s naked chest.*

Virgil (*together*)   Why did you . . . out of the blue?

Alice (*together*)   Sorry, it's the middle of the night.

Virgil   What?

Alice   What? Sorry . . . I . . . (*Pause.*) How are you?

Virgil (*a faint laugh. Pause*)   Listen, when did we last speak?

Alice   I don't know. My mother's funeral, I think.

Virgil   Yes, eight months ago. And we didn't speak, by the way, you just left a message.

Alice   Oh. I'm sorry. I need to talk to you.

Virgil   Why?

Alice   I just do. Something's happened. Something very strange.

Pause.

Virgil   Are you going to tell me why you did what you did?

Alice   It's difficult. I don't know where to begin. After my mother's funeral, well, her cremation . . .

Virgil   So no vultures then?

Alice   Sorry?

Virgil   Doesn't matter.

Alice   Anyway, after her funeral, I know that I took that money from our account, the £2,000. I know, I know it was everything. I was so . . . well, I took a train to Paris.

Scene Seventeen

The video image freezes and disappears. SFX – Train. It thunders through her voice and we are in the Eurostar train. She is looking out of the window. **Virgil** *is listening on his mobile.*

Alice (*VO*)   She told me my father was dead. She always told me my father was dead. The one time I asked her about the card which came for her every Christmas, the one time I asked her about it . . . she never said a thing.

Virgil *stands in the middle of his room.*

Alice (*VO*)   Changed in Paris and took a night train to Berlin.

Virgil*'s room inverts. The chairs are carried SR across to where the bed is. The bed glides over* **Virgil***, who is now lying down, with* **Alice** *lying on it, as if on a couchette on its way to Berlin.*

Alice (*VO*)   She died. She never said a thing. Never said a thing.

It was her sister who told me my father was alive. Could be alive. Might be living. Somewhere.

The bed is still moving above **Virgil** *who lies beneath it.* **Alice** *in the sleeping compartment.*

Alice (*VO*)   He met my mother one autumn on the Baltic coast near Klaipeda, Lithuania. 1962. It was late summer. Late summer. Klaipeda, Lithuania . . . Lithuania.

I know nothing about him. I have no objects belonging to him. All I have is a wind-up watch, Russian-made, which I found wrapped in yellowing paper at the bottom of one of my mother's study drawers. Broken. Broken.

She lies down and goes to sleep. **Virgil** *lays his head on the stone DSC.*

Scene Eighteen

Spindler *and a group of* **Scientists**.

Spindler   A broken stick. Splinters of wood. Strips of leather. Scraps of hide. Fur. Tufts of twisted grass. Fragments of bark. Two round objects on a piece of twine.

Scientist 3   A broken stick.

Scientist 2   Splinters of wood.

Scientist 1   Strips of leather.

Scientist 4   Fur.

Spindler   Tufts of twisted grass.

Scientist 4   Fragments of bark.

Scientist 1   Two round objects on a piece of twine.

Spindler *and* **Scientists** *examine objects on the mountainside.* **Virgil** *gets up and, as if following his conversation, makes circles on the floor where the Iceman dropped his equipment.*

Spindler   A broken stick which was found here (*SFX – wind*) up on this ledge where the Iceman must have placed it on his way down to the gully. We imagine he came this way to this rock because we found some of his equipment, which was made of birch bark, just here. Some of it was pulverized, possibly by the feet of tourists as they came to look at the body. And this is where two splinters of bone were left. Possibly spat out because this is where he laid his head, on this stone. All of these things were left exactly where he dropped them or placed them 5,000 years ago when he came up here to this lonely place and lay down on his left and died. Now, he lay on his left side for a very specific reason.

Virgil *puts the mobile to his ear. SFX – Screech of train wheels.*

Scene Nineteen

Alice (*VO*)   Berlin.

She leaves the train and collides with a woman on the platform. Her bag falls and the woman helps her pick it up. They shake hands and part. **Virgil** *moves across the stage, on the phone.*

Virgil   What?

The woman collides with her again. Same result.

Virgil   What?

This happens exactly the same again. After this **Alice** *hurtles CS and everyone moves round her as if on the streets of Berlin. She is accosted by a ranting* **East Berliner**.

Berlin Man   Jetzt wo de Mauer weg is, wees ja keener, wo er hinjehört. Jetzt kommen se alle zurück, die Idioten, mit Jeld in der Tasche, bauen se uns Klötze vor de Tür. Kuck de doch nur mal den Potsdamer Platz an! Da kriegste ja keene Sonne mehr im Jesicht. Berlin, Berlin! Was is denn det jeworden? Lichtenberg . . . Köpenick, da kannte ick eenen, dem seene Zeene haben se ihm alle rausjeschlagen. Ja und ick? Wo soll ick hin jetzt, bin doch hier jeboren.

Ist doch alles nur Scheisse jetzt, ist doch nur Scheisse.

Another man laughs hysterically. A woman begs. Men move their chairs around **Alice** *until they have created a cafe. She sits.*

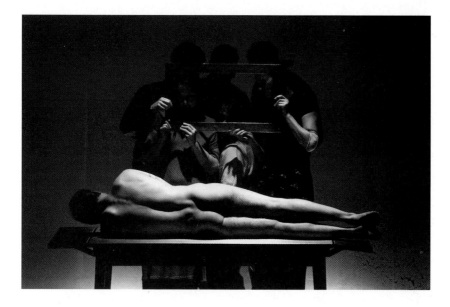

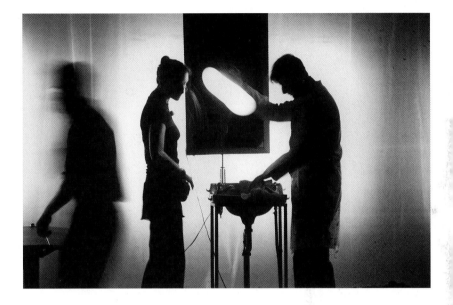

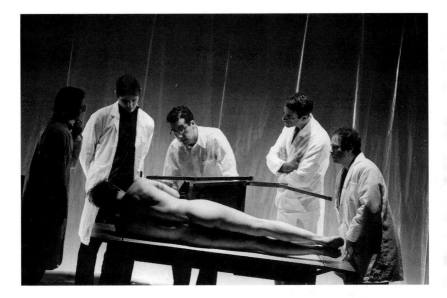

Alice   Einen café, bitte.

She turns to look at the men beside her. They suddenly put homburgs on their heads.

Alice (*VO*)   Started looking at men over sixty in a different way. Was he ever on the Baltic coast?

The men remove their homburgs as she looks away. Waiter returns with the coffee. She can't find her purse. She searches desperately, hoping that it isn't stolen.

Alice   Shit. Fuck, fuck.

Virgil *stands and makes his way to bed.* **Alice** *looks up and remembers. We see again the moment when the woman stole it.*

Alice (*shouts*)   No.

She moves towards the bed. Cross-fade to the sound of a hotel room. **Virgil** *is sitting in the bed. She undresses and gets into bed. As she gets into it he gets out. Their movements mirror one another. She looks at her father's watch.*

Alice (*VO*)   Was he ever on the Baltic coast?

Scene Twenty

Virgil *shakes his head, disbelieving.*

Virgil (*muttering into the phone*)   You.

The scene cuts to the archaeological laboratory.

Spindler   Yew.

Scientist 1   Lime.

Scientist 2   Ash.

Scientist 3   Hazel.

Scientist 4   Birch.

Spindler   Norway spruce.

Scientist 1   Blackthorn.

Spindler   The Iceman had seventeen types of wood on or about his person when he died. Seventeen. The broken stick. One metre eighty-two in height.

Scientist 4   A bow.

Spindler   And near it a quiver.

Virgil *is sitting CS holding his mobile. By chance, almost, it forms the central strut of the shape of a bow the others form with their fragments of wood.*

Scientist 4   Arrows.

Spindler   A Neolithic bow, had a force of up to forty kilograms. At fifty metres the arrow would pass straight through you.

The **Scientists** *form images with the fragments of wood, moving them like arrows.*

Spindler   The boards of wood.

Scientist 1   A back pannier.

They form the shape of a back pannier on **Virgil***'s body.*

Spindler   A wooden-framed back pannier still used in parts of Europe in the twentieth century. Fur.

Scientist 3   A hat.

Spindler   The strips of leather.

Scientist 2   Leggings. Trousers.

Spindler   The fit was loose, allowing room to bend and climb. Strips of hide.

Scientist 2   A pouch.

Spindler   And in the pouch . . .

Scientist 2   Fire-lighting equipment.

Alice *sits up, pulls a cigarette from her bag and lights it.* **Virgil** *mirrors this in front of the TV DSR.*

Spindler   Matches. And the fragments of bark.

Scientist 4   Birch bark.

Scientist 1   A cylindrical container.

Spindler   A box.

Scientist 4   Blackish inside . . .

Spindler   Containing . . .

Scientist 4   Norway Maple leaves with flakes of charcoal.

Spindler   This must have been a vessel for carrying live embers. And the two round objects on a piece of twine.

Scientist 2   Birch fungus.

Spindler   Five thousand years before the discovery of penicillin.

Scientist 2   A natural antibiotic.

Spindler   A travelling medicine kit. Seventeen types of wood, seventeen. Each perfectly suited to its task. He was complete. Where was he going?

Virgil (*VO*)   How many mourned him when he disappeared? He has gone to the mountain, is that what they said? How many songs did he know? What made him laugh repeatedly? How did he imagine immortality? For imagine it he did.

Virgil *sitting by the TV speaks to* **Alice** *on his mobile.*

Virgil   Jesus, where did you think you were going? What were you doing?

Alice*, in the bed, turns in her sleep violently.*

Scene Twenty-one

A **Maid** *bangs on* **Alice***'s door. She doesn't wake. The* **Maid** *explodes into the room and speaking quickly and aggressively attempts to get her out of there.*

Maid   Aufmachen. Aufmachen, bitte.

Alice   Er . . . fünf minute . . . bitte . . . fünf minute . . .

Maid   In fünf minuten müssen Sie für das Zimmer bezahlen . . .

Alice   Christ . . . ein . . . ein . . . Entschuldigung.

Maid   Ja, ja, Entschuldigung, Entschuldigung, ich werde Probleme haben. Ach du heiliger Strohsack. Was ist denn das fur einen Treck? Schnee im Zimmer? Das glaube ich nicht . . . Donnerwetter!

The **Maid** *is trying to make the bed and clean the room.*

Alice   Fünf minutes.

Maid   Nein, nein . . .

Alice *(attempting to tidy the bed)*   Ich helfen du . . .

Maid   Ne touchez pas ce lit! Elle m'énerve la touriste.

Alice   Ah, vous parlez français?

Maid   Oui.

Alice   Oui. Je peux mieux m'éxpliquer en francais. Ecoutez, je suis desolée. Alors c'est une jour terrible pour moi, hier, on m'a volé toute mon argent . . .

Maid   C'est Berlin ici, Madame: on fait attention! C'est plein d'étrangers! C'est une plaque tournante: il y a que des immigrants, les Polonais, les Russes, les Juifs . . .

Alice   Oui, et des Français aussi!

Maid   Quoi des Français? Je suis Allemande, moi, Madame!

Alice   Mais vous parlez tres bien Français pour une Allemande.

Maid   Oh . . . c'est à dire je suis venue, je me suis mariée et puis . . . et puis de quoi je me mèle? Vous êtes de la police? Vous voulez voir mes papiers?

Alice   Non, non. Doucement, doucement. J'ai dit que je suis desolée. Alors calme . . .

Maid   Je suis calme! C'est à vous ça?

The **Maid** discovers her watch among the bedclothes. The **Maid** drops the watch on the floor. **Virgil** picks it up and leads **Alice** to the taxi.

Scene Twenty-two

Alice *is in a taxi. She's trying to get her watch to work. The driver is in front.*

Simonides   Where are we going?

Alice   Waterloo International, please.

Simonides   Eurostar. Yes. OK.

Alice (*shaking her watch*)   Shit.

Simonides   Are you talking to me?

Alice   No. Sorry. This watch. It's stopped.

Simonides   Oh, do you want me to take a look?

Alice   It's very old. It's delicate.

All right. Just a look. Trust me.

Alice   Do you know about watches?

Simonides   Yes, yes, I know everything about watches.

He pulls over, fiddles with the watch.

Oh, it's very beautiful, very old (*Laughing*.) marvellous.

Alice   Do you know where it's from?

Simonides   Of course, it's a communist watch. From the Soviet Union.

Alice   It's Russian.

Simonides   Yes. It's wonderful. Very nice. Very simple. It needs only a regulation. I can fix it in a minute.

Alice   Thank you very much.

Simonides   You're welcome.

Alice   Where are you from?

Simonides   Me? I am from Islington.

Alice   No, no . . . I mean originally.

Simonides   Oh, Greece. There you go. It works now.

Alice   Thank you.

Simonides   Welcome. And you? Where are you from?

*Virgil takes **Alice**'s place in the taxi.*

Spindler   He was travelling north.

Simonides (*to **Virgil***)   And you? Where are you from?

Alice *gazes out.* **Virgil** *looks up. A moment of suspension.*

Scene Twenty-three

Cut back to the hotel room. **Alice** *grabs her watch from the floor and puts it to her ear.*

Alice   Fuck! Oh, no!

Maid   Merde!

Alice   It's stopped. Vous êtes une fucking stupid woman.

Maid   You speak English?

Alice   Yes, I speak English.

Maid   You are English!

Alice   No. I'm a Welsh Lithuanian from north fucking London. Do you want to see my passport?

Maid   No, no.

Alice   Alors, c'est cassé! Oui. Cassé. Voilà!

Maid   Oh, merde, y'faut vraiment que ça m'arrive à moi ca'!

She taps the watch on the headboard of the bed.

Alice   Don't do that!

Maid   Please, you don't tell the manager!

Alice   I'm not going to tell the management.

Maid   But you promise because it's also your fault!

Alice   I'm not going to tell the management. Just give it back to me . . .

Maid   Because if I lose this job I'm back on the street.

Alice   It's important. Give it back.

Maid   Groß Berlin, big trouble . . .

Alice   It belonged to my father.

We are back in **Simonides***'s taxi.*

Simonides   And to his father before him. My grandfather. Now they are mine. They are worry beads, but personally I have no worries, they are just to kill the time. I'm going straight here, I think it's better, isn't it? You know my worry beads are not Greek, they're Turkish. My grandfather was a refugee from Turkey. He was speaking Turkish better than Greek, I speak Greek better than English and my son, he speaks English better than Greek.

Here is my little boy. He looks like his mother but only the face because inside he's like me.

Back in the hotel room.

Maid   He gave it to you?

Alice   No.

Maid   He's dead?

Alice   No, no . . . he's not dead. I'm looking for him.

Maid   Ah voilà. He left? Il a quitté vot' mère, et par conséquent il vous a quitté aussi! Ah les hommes, c'est bien tous les mêmes!

Alice (*more definite*)   No. It's more complicated than that.

Maid   Non, non, c'est pas complicated. The men: one day they are here, one day they disappear. It is like that. I know, je connais ça.

Alice   It's not what you think.

Maid   Moi, quand mon mari m'a quitté, c'était dur. Pas seulement pour moi: c'était dur pour ma fille. Regardez: ma p'tite she looks exactly like her father. Only the face, though. She is completely different inside, she's like me. When my husband left she did not understand, only suffering. You have to forget the past.

Alice   Thank you. I know what I'm doing.

Maid   Yes, especially when you get your wallet stolen in Berlin? In the past, you always arrive too late. Too late. Don't go back, go home.

Scene Twenty-four

The **Scientists** *examine the Iceman's objects. The detail of their work is picked out on a television screen and projected on to the bed.*

Spindler   He was travelling north. The glowing embers in his birch-bark container were kept warm by a layer of insulating leaves, leaves from the Norway maple which 5,000 years ago grew only on the southern slopes of the Alps. So he must have been travelling north.

Scientist   The condition of the leaves is so good that chlorophyll can still be extracted with alcohol.

Scientist   They are still green.

Spindler   Freshly picked.

Scientist   And on the leaves traces of corn. Recently threshed.

Spindler   So he came from the lowlands.

Scientist   And he left after the harvest.

Spindler   It was the onset of winter.

Scientist   Analysis of the leaves reveals six different types of wood which he used as fuel.

Spindler   Taken from the lowlands to beyond the edge of the treeline.

Scientist   Analysis of his stomach contents show that he had not eaten for twelve or more hours.

Spindler   A man leaves his valley with almost no food.

Scientist   He lights fires at different altitudes.

Scientist   As he climbs the mountain.

Scientist   He was travelling fast.

Spindler   He was an experienced mountaineer. Why would he put himself in that position? What was he doing with no food at 3,000 metres at the onset of winter? What was he doing?

Virgil and **Alice** are on the telephone.

Virgil   So, why didn't you?

Alice   What?

Virgil   For Christ's sake. Just do what she said. Come home.

Scene Twenty-five

An instant cut to a train crossing central Europe where Alice is talking with two **American Tourists** *and a* **Polish Man**.

American   . . . in Minnesota . . . two years there and then we moved on to Rapid City and so now we live in Baltimore. I said to Trudi, we've moved dozens of times in our lives, for God's sake now we've gotta make our journey to Europe, you know, really to find, well, to trace our . . .

Polish Man   You American?

American   Yes . . . you want a cookie . . . ahh . . . wahlen sie einen Biscuit? Sprechen sie Deutsch?

Polish Man   Niet . . . Polski. (*He takes a biscuit.*) Thank you very much.

American   Yes, what the hell, you're welcome, buddy. (*Back to* **Alice**.) We've been in Europe for about three weeks now. We've seen just about everything. Paris, Rome, Amsterdam, Edinburgh. Edinburgh is such a beautiful place. But Baltimore is a terrific place also, downtown, you know, they've completely renovated, there's nobody there any more, it's great . . . we live right outside . . . (*He carries on talking but is silent.*)

Alice (*VO*)   . . . and so in Berlin my money was taken. Everything gone, everything except my passport. But I had to go on. Got a job in a bar in Bahnhofstrasse.

A brief image of a bar appears and then disappears.

Went every day to the office where you trace people, you know, the branch of the police, what is it called? Der something something. Nobody knew where he was. But I found out there was a sister-in-law in Warsaw.

American   . . . the Warsaw ghetto, so, uh, Trudi really liked the ghetto museum. I found it a little disturbing . . .

Alice   So why did you go?

American   Well, we had family.

Alice   . . . sorry, I'm so . . .

American   No, it's all right, it's difficult, really difficult. Anyway, next, we're going on to Treblinka . . .

Polish Man   Treblinka.

American   . . . Yes, you know, we're doing a kind of pilgrimage, basically following the trail . . . (*He carries on talking silently.*)

Scene Twenty-six

Alice *pulls out a spoon. She looks at it. A fast cut to the sitting room of a Polish flat in Warsaw. She is given a bowl of soup. In the same room* **Four Students** *watch a game of football. An international match.*

Alice (*VO*)   Arrive in Warsaw.

The Sister-in-law talks to the students about the game and then addresses **Alice** *in Polish, asking about herself.*

Sister-in-law   Alicya.

Alice   Alice.

Sister-in-law   Co się stalo?

Student   Nie było gola.

Sister-in-law   Nie było gola, o, niech to szlag!

Alice   Dobre . . . dobre zupa.

Sister-in-law   Typowa polska zupa. Smakowało? Tak, bardzo smączna. Skąd jesteś, dziecko? Skąd. Jesteś. Dziecko?

Alice   I don't understand.

Alice (*VO*)   Sister-in-law says . . .

Sister-in-law   Where are you come from?

Alice *looks out thinking about the question. Two other memories crowd in. The minicab driver and another character we have not yet met. These scenes take place either side of her.*

Simonides   Greece.

Doctor   Switzerland.

In the taxi.

Simonides   But I don't miss it. I sold the house and left my country many years ago. And first I went to Germany. Worked in a fucking watch factory.

Doctor (*starts speaking in Swiss*)   Sorry, I slipped into my own language.

Simonides   After this. Then I came here in London. As you see I work as a minicab driver.

Doctor   I don't know if I can help you. I've only been here for three weeks. I work for the International Red Cross.

Simonides   I don't look back, you know this is the first rule for a taxi driver, don't look back or you will have a crash. No, my friend, I am interested in what is in front of me. I believe in the future.

*The **Students** cheer. A goal is almost scored. Cross-fade to the flat. The Polish woman mysteriously hands her a box, indicating that it is hers. The woman takes her by the hand and leads her to another room in the flat. **Virgil** crosses DSR to television.*

Alice *(VO)*   She shows me a bedroom in her flat where he used to lodge when he was a student. She gives me a box of his things. A scarf. A lighter. A pair of old shoes. He had small feet.

She enters the bleak bedroom and looks out of the window.

Alice *(VO)*   She hasn't heard from him for twenty years but she gives me the name of a friend in Riga.

Was he ever on the Baltic coast?

She opens the box.

Scene Twenty-seven

SFX – Train cuts the scene. **Alice** *sits with a single man, a BBC foreign correspondent.*

Alice *(trying to remember)*   Well, she wrote down the name of the friend. It's Andrei . . . er . . . Preznez . . . *(Gives up and refers to a piece of paper in the box.)* Andrei Preznezknek.

BBC Man *(takes paper)*   Preznezkniac. Preznezkniac. I think you'll find the k is silent.

Alice *(taking things out of the box given to her by the Polish woman)* Shoes.

BBC Man   He's a motor cyclist. Well, look at the way the right is worn more than the left. Here and here.

Alice   A lighter.

BBC Man   He's a smoker.

Alice   Brilliant. And a rather beautiful scarf.

BBC Man   That shouldn't be in there with a pair of shoes and a lighter, it's disrespectful.

Alice   What do you mean?

BBC Man   It's a tallith.

Alice   No, no it's my father's scarf.

BBC Man   No, it's a tallith.

Alice   A what?

BBC Man   A tallith. A prayer shawl. May I?

He shows her the four corners of the shawl.

These represent the four corners of the world . . . and the knots are the Ten Commandments . . . I think . . . Well, that's what I was told. It's been a long time. I haven't been to a synagogue since I was a child. Your father is a Jew.

They change seats holding the scarf between them. As they cross, the **Scientists** *hold out the fragments of wood in the shape of the bow.*

Spindler   With a little more work the bow would have become an effective weapon but he was not granted the time to complete it. Why had he not completed the bow before he climbed the mountain? His labours must have been disturbed.

When seated, he takes the scarf and carefully folds it. She offers him some paper. He gently kisses the scarf. He wraps the scarf in the paper and places it in her bag.

Alice   So, I just feel that if I don't have a past, I can't relate to people now.

BBC Man (*referring to the stone around her neck*)   What's this?

Alice   What? Oh, it's just a piece of stone. It's nothing really.

BBC Man   Sorry, you were saying.

Alice   Yes, if I can't live in the present, I certainly can't fucking imagine the future.

BBC Man   You're carrying five thousand years of history, struggle, migration and stories.

Alice   I'm sorry?

BBC Man   It's inside you . . . wherever you go . . . as a Jew.

Alice   No, no, you've completely misunderstood me.

They change seats looking at each other as they change. The **Scientists** *change US. They form the shape of the box around* **Virgil***'s cigarette.*

Spindler   The birch-bark container, with the comfort from its hot embers, was the last thing that slipped from his fingers. He was exhausted. He had been travelling fast.

Alice   So, you're saying, as a Jew, you hate all Jews.

BBC Man   No, I'm saying that, as a Jew, I find Jewish people increasingly impossible to live with.

Alice   That's not what you were saying before.

BBC Man   That is exactly what I said five minutes ago, if you were listening.

Alice   So what you're really saying is you can't live with yourself.

BBC Man   He plays the piano.

Alice   What?

BBC Man   Your father, he plays the piano. The shoe is worn here and here . . . the pedal . . . maybe he was pianist.

They change seats, looking more closely at each other as they change. The fragments of wood close in on them from all angles.

Spindler   The bow was unfinished. His quiver was broken. He was carrying the broken pieces as though he had snatched them up in a hurry. Which tells us that he was running, but what was he running from?

BBC Man (*looking out of the window*)   Across the whole of Europe, thousands of people running for their lives . . .

Alice   . . . a mass migration . . .

BBC Man   Yes, before the twentieth century has even begun. They crossed these fields, passed through these villages. It's a great story if you think about it. My four grandparents, all born in different countries. Stuffing a dozen things in a duffel bag and fleeing for their lives. And in a new country finding love, hope and happiness. It's a beautiful story, an epic story. I just don't know the details. (*Pause.*) You know, I never bothered to ask. It's too late now.

Disturbed at his own words he looks at his reflection in the train window. **Alice** *leans forward and attempts to touch him. He senses and turns, laughing.*

BBC Man   But I could teach you a song. An old Yiddish drinking song that my grandfather taught me. It's the only cultural baggage I've got. Well, that and the guilt. It's a long journey and we've got nothing better to do . . .

Alice   Go on, then.

BBC Man   Believe it or not, it begins with oy.

Alice   Oy.

BBC Man   Yes, oy.

Alice   Oy!

BBC Man   No, don't send it up.

He teaches her the song and they both sing. The company join in. As they sing everyone begins to cross the stage from SR to SL. As they do so we should be reminded of refugees carrying bags, blankets, chairs. **Simonides** *steps behind them, he is in his taxi. The singing continues. As he speaks,* **Alice** *and the* **BBC Man** *face each other across the bed. He removes his clothes. She does too.* **Virgil** *is between them. We do not know if it is for real or in* **Virgil***'s imagination.* **Alice** *outlines the man's naked body with her hand.* **Virgil** *almost brushes them as he comes off the bed. They lie down.*

Simonides   Always moving from east to west. Always running from other fucking people. My grandparents were Greek refugees from Turkey. In 1922 they were expelled, they had to flee. Thousands of people were in the ports, running from the Turkish soldiers, waiting for the boats. My grandmother was on the gangplank. She carried her baby in one arm and a watermelon in the other. The only thing she says, everybody was pushing and shouting. She was so confused. And this soldier was shouting at her face, 'One item only, you are allowed one object only. Throw this thing away.' So she threw the watermelon away. She gets on the boat and she realizes that instead of throwing the watermelon she threw the baby. But you know, this is the past, my friend. I'm going left here, I think it's better. I'm going to emigrate again. Next year I'm going to Melbourne, Australia. And after this, who knows, maybe California and before I die I will get my body frozen so I will wake up stark naked in a better life.

Alice *is in bed with the* **BBC Man**. **Virgil** *lies on the table USC, in despair.*

Alice   What does nakedness remind us of? Dear God, what does nakedness remind us of?

Scene Twenty-eight

Spindler   The Iceman was not naked when he died. His cloak was made from very long grasses. For a man who spent prolonged periods in the wilderness, the construction is marvellous. It is easily put on and taken off. While resting it could be used as a ground sheet or, at night, a blanket. Such grass is highly water repellent. For a hunter, moreover, it would provide excellent camouflage. Such a cloak is the mark of an experienced mountaineer. That's what he was, an experienced mountaineer.

As **Spindler** *speaks,* **Virgil** *gets off the table, goes to the bed where the lovers are.* **Alice** *and the* **BBC Man** *at once stand up, move as if taking off their clothes another time, and again collapse on to the bed.* **Virgil** *stands in his room lost for a moment, and then lies on the stone. These movements are repeated like pictures that replay themselves* *in the sleepless mind, over and over at four in the morning. Only the text changes.*

Again **Virgil** *moves from the table, repeating the pattern of movement which continues throughout the following speech. The bed . . . the room . . . falling on the stone . . . the death.*

Spindler   All expeditions to the high mountains must be well provisioned. A supply of food is essential. Two small splinters of Ibex bone were found at the base of the rock shelf, close to the dying man. Only splinters, the meat must have been gnawed off. Possibly, given that he had no stored fat reserves, he had been subjected, before his death, to an involuntary starvation diet. The splinter that he had set down was his last piece of meat. He was starving. He was starving.

Again the same movements return.

X-rays of the body show rib fractures testifying to his violent life. On the left side the fifth, sixth, seventh and ninth ribs showed healed fractures. All five had healed well. But on the right side, the third, fourth, fifth and sixth are broken and somewhat out of position. There is no sign of calcification. No trace of bones having healed. This is why he lay on his left because his ribs were broken. That is why he lay on his left.

And again the actions are repeated.

Taken altogether, this suggests that the Iceman suffered a disaster. A fight with hostile humans or a fight with wild animals. What seems very odd, however, is that he took with him only some of his equipment. There was time only for a semi-orderly retreat. This would suggest that his presumed adversary did not force him into headlong flight but, nevertheless, made him leave the scene in something of a hurry. These reflections narrow down his opponents to human beings. That is what he was running from. Cold, in pain, hungry, pursued. He was fleeing from a danger, a disaster which had provoked him to risk his own life.

Virgil (*VO*)   How many children did he have? What word did he use to signify summer . . . or this place? How many songs did he know? Had he yet heard the story of the flood?

Virgil *slowly picks up his phone.*

Virgil   So how old was he?

Alice   What?

Virgil   What colour was his hair?

Alice   What colour was his hair?

Virgil   Yes.

Alice   I don't know. Brown, nine centimetres long, why do you want to know? . . . look, for God's sake, it doesn't matter.

Virgil   Who was he?

Alice   Oh, just some guy I met on the train. He works for the BBC, he's an Eastern Europe correspondent or something. I don't know.

Virgil   And did you . . .

Alice   . . . no. We didn't.

Virgil   No, I mean, did you not think he might be having you on?

Alice   What?

Virgil   Your father. Maybe he was given it.

Alice   What?

Virgil   The tallith. Maybe someone gave it to him.

BBC Man (*looking at her necklace*)   I know what it is. It's palaganite. Do you know it's 400 million years old. Give or take the odd fifty million years or so. Mind you, Newtonian time is totally irrelevant. Twenty-four hours is just a human construct, it doesn't exist outside of us. How long is a day? It all depends on how you . . .

Alice   Would you like it?

BBC Man   What?

Alice   Would you like it?

BBC Man   Really?

Alice   Yes, it's too heavy.

BBC Man   Thanks. Do you have the right time?

Alice   No, my watch is broken.

BBC Man   Well, anyway, what is time after all? A very interesting subject. I made a programme about it, it got some good reviews. Maybe you saw it?

Alice   No. I didn't.

BBC Man   The idea of the Newtonian universe, a clockwork universe, is totally irrelevant. The universe is chaotic, a series of patterns, repeating, over and over, it's shifting constantly but repeating in the most complex . . .

Alice *has packed her bags, left him and is talking to* **Virgil**. *Their conversation immediately becomes an argument.*

The sound of a train.

Scene Twenty-nine

Alice *holds her head in her hands, puts on her sunglasses and gazes out of the window.* **Virgil** *mirrors this beside her, in his room.*

Alice (*VO*)   When I get to Riga I take work in a bar. Another fucking bar. This time completely illegally. No papers.

The bar in Riga. DS plastic curtain is pulled across. We see people dancing. A man is seated CS. **Alice** *sits on him, her top body towards the plastic.* **Virgil** *is DS of the plastic curtain smoking a cigarette with one hand almost against the plastic curtain.*

Alice (*VO*)   But I track down the friend. An old drunk man. Tells me again and again how I look like him. Same hair too, he says, fingering mine.

Virgil *and* **Alice** *are still separated by the film of the plastic.*

Alice (*VO*)   He tells me jokes all the time. When I laugh, he says, I first heard that one from your father. Again and again and again . . . but I learn I have a half-brother who lives in Kiev. Maybe he's in the Ukraine now.

South to Kiev. 1,300 miles.

Everyone crosses the stage, SL to SR, the reverse of the refugees. The television flickers into life. Bodies move behind the plastic.

News Broadcast (*from the newsroom of the BBC World Service*) The remains of a Neolithic man thought to be more than 5,000 years old have arrived at a museum in northern Italy after a journey from Austria in a refrigerated truck.

While **Virgil** *listens to the broadcast the bodies behind the plastic lie down on their chairs, their positions at once suggesting the position of the Iceman and dead bodies in a mortuary.*

The body was moved amid tight security following a threat of unspecified terrorist action by an underground Austrian nationalist group.

We see the bodies that look almost as if they are suspended in space.

Alice (*VO*)   Kiev. Where I find my half-brother who works in forensic medicine. He says:

On the TV, DSR, the close-up of a pair of teeth appear.

Half-brother   Alice, you'd be surprised how much teeth can tell you about a life.

The TV image pulls back to reveal the face of **Spindler**.

Spindler   The teeth of the Iceman are ground down through chewing rather in the manner of a modern-day pipe smoker and the degree of abrasion suggests that he was aged between thirty-five and . . .

Virgil   He was forty years old when he died.

Spindler   Which, in the Neolithic period, would have made him an old man.

The image cuts out. Spotlight on **Alice**.

Alice (*VO*)   He gives me a cassette, my father playing the piano, five years ago, New Year's Eve.

The bodies sit up for a moment, briefly evoking the position of a piano player.

Where is he now? My half-brother doesn't know, but he gives me the name of a hospital near Tarnow in Galicia, Poland, Poland, Poland . . .

Virgil *is on the phone.*

Virgil   A hospital in Poland? My God, what was that like?

An **Orderly** *in a white coat sweeps across to reveal a hospital. He stops by a patient.*

Alice   Where are you from?

She stands up and walks into the hospital.

Scene Thirty

Doctor   Switzerland. (*He speaks Swiss German.*) It's complete chaos here. We have people from everywhere.

Alice   I can't understand you.

Doctor   Sorry, I slipped into my own language. I don't know if I can help you. I've only been here for three weeks. I work for the International Red Cross. It's complete chaos here. We have people from all over Eastern Europe.

Alice   Please try.

Doctor   Well, there is a woman who has been here for more than a year, maybe she knows something. What was your father's name again?

The noise level obliterates **Alice***'s reply. The* **Doctor** *clears the plastic and we are in the hospital. The* **Doctor** *leans over an imaginary invalid, a bed rushes into position, revealing an old woman propped up on the pillows.*

The **Doctor** *speaks to her in German asking questions. Throughout the following text, she whispers her reply.* **Alice** *gestures with her father's belongings.*

Doctor   She doesn't know the name.

Alice   Shit.

Doctor   Can you tell her anything else about him?

Alice   Well, he looked a bit like me. Same hair. Well, it would be grey. He smoked. He played the piano, a jazz pianist. He told a lot of jokes. Maybe she'd remember that.

Some more explanation.

Alice   What did she say?

Doctor   Apparently there was a man who fits your father's description.

A man comes in and takes away her father's shoe.

Alice   When did he leave? Does she know when he left?

Doctor   Five or six months ago. She's not sure.

Orderly   Doctor. Scand ona yiest? (Where's she from?)

Doctor   London.

Orderly   London. Buckingham Palace. Big Ben.

Doctor   Apparently he had a bad accident.

Alice   An accident?

Doctor   Yes, he broke a few ribs.

A man comes in and takes away her father's lighter. The situation is getting out of control.

Alice   Well, is he alive? Is my father alive? Does she know?

Doctor   One morning he just got up and left. He must have discharged himself.

Orderly   London. Fish and chips.

Alice   Yes. Yes. Where is he now? Does she know where he is now?

Doctor   Yes. She does.

A man comes in and takes away her father's tallith.

Doctor   She knows the name of a place called Moklavic.

Alice   Moklavic?

Orderly   Moklavic.

Doctor   It's a village about two or three hours away from here.

Alice   A village?

Orderly   Village people.

Alice   Well, how do I get there?

Doctor   Do you have a car?

Alice   No, no. I don't have a car.

Doctor   Vitek can take you now, if you want to go. Do you want to go? He can take you now, straight away.

The noise rises. **Alice** *tries to get her belongings back. The bed slides sideways as* **Virgil** *moves CS. The break-up of the scene mirrors the voice breaking up over the mobile.*

Virgil   Alice. Alice. You're breaking up.

Scene Thirty-one

Noise cuts.

Virgil *(VO)*   Alice? Alice? Shit, you've gone completely.
Hello, hello. Alice, I can't hear you any more. Maybe you
can hear me. Alice, Alice come back on, come back on. Still
can't hear you, still can't hear you. I'll keep talking just in
case you can hear me, feel like an idiot. Alice, oh fuck, if you
can hear me, forget everything I've said, I really want you to
call me back . . . please.

*He looks at the phone. He switches on the TV. He plunges his head in
water and puts the phone on the table, looking at it intently. He takes
the chair and scrutinizes the TV to kill time, clutching the telephone.
He changes channels and starts to dream.*

Montage *(VO)*   Early in 1938 engineers of the American
electronics company Westinghouse Electrics decided that
the technology had arrived that would enable them to create
a time capsule capable of lasting 5,000 years, a period which
roughly equates with recorded history. They believed that
they could overcome the major problems that arise in such a
project: how to construct a vessel that would not perish, how
to make sure it would be found so far in the future and what
to put in it that would be truly representative of twentieth-
century civilization. They decided that . . .

. . . a fairly substantial sample of human hair was recovered
from the upper edge of the grass cloak; dark brown, black,
curly about nine centimetres long. And in view of his age we
may assume he was balding.

He was balding.

It is highly likely he had a beard.

He had a beard.

And the individual strands of hair point to the fact that he
wore his hair loose, not plaited into pigtails or knotted.

He wore his hair loose.

Same hair too, he says, fingering mine.

The dead man's skin is now leathery and tough.

Where is he now?

He lay on his left.

She shows me a room in her flat where he used to lodge as a student.

His head was resting on a boulder. A boulder. He lay down on his left side.

He had small feet.

For five thousand years his feet were lying one on top of the other. He lay to the side of the glacier, so that in five thousand years the forces in the ice turned him only through ninety degrees.

The four corners of the earth. A piano player. A lighter. A scarf.

A cloak made from twisted grasses. He lay on the rocky ground, fully clothed.

Virgil *looks at the stone. He lifts it, the company fall to the floor. As he moves the stone, the company turn as if in the ice. He replaces the stone and the company stand up and continue towards their final positions.*

Montage (*VO*)   His objects remained where he left them . . .

A wind-up watch, Russian-made.

. . . or where they fell from his hand.

Broken. Broken.

Virgil *picks up the chair. It begins to fall apart and he puts it on the table.*

Montage (*VO*)   It is quite possible for two or three metres of snow to fall in a single night and snow takes between ten and twenty years to turn into ice.

Virgil (*VO*)   And so we can attempt a reconstruction . . .

Alice (*VO*)   Started looking at men over sixty in a different way.

Virgil *begins to move the chair. It suggests an arm, a leg, gestures.*

Montage (*VO*)   What was an old man . . .

What was an old man, with arthritic pain . . .

What was an old man, with arthritic pain and broken ribs doing . . .

What was an old man, with arthritic pain and broken ribs doing at that altitude . . .

What was an old man, with arthritic pain and broken ribs doing at that altitude with no food at the beginning of winter?

Where are you going?

Was he ever on the Baltic coast?

Where is he now? Where is he now?

Where are you going? What are you running from?

Where is he now?

Scene Thirty-two

The phone rings.

Virgil   Alice . . . Alice, is that you?

Pause. The sound of **Alice** *crying.*

Virgil   Alice, what's happened?

Alice   I need your help.

Virgil   Well, tell me what's happened, what happened after the hospital?

Alice   I can't remember.

Virgil   What?

Alice   I don't remember.

Virgil   What do you mean?

Alice   I just know that there was a car journey. It was cold. There were trees. And I was on a train here.

Virgil   A train? Where?

Alice   I'm in some grotty hotel.

Virgil   Where?

Alice   I just had to get out of there. Everywhere I'd been was so flat I needed to get to the mountains.

Virgil   The mountains? Where?

Alice   I'm in northern Italy.

Virgil   Jesus. Northern Italy? What's the name of the place?

Alice   It's just a small town. Bolzano.

Virgil   Bolzano. I know it.

Alice   You do?

Virgil   Yes.

Alice   Why?

Virgil   It's where the Iceman is . . .

Alice   Who?

Virgil   The Iceman, in his refrigeration unit. Listen, it doesn't matter.

Alice   No, just keep talking, tell me about him. I need to hear your voice.

Virgil   OK. Well, don't you remember, they found his body in 1991 up on the Austrian–Italian border and he was supposed to be 5,000 years old? And he went up the mountain and was caught in a storm and froze to death. They even thought he might be running from something. God, there are so many theories . . .

Alice   Well, tell me them.

Scene Thirty-three

Applause. The company sit in a line DS. They are delegates for a conference. They mime earplugs that give them a simultaneous translation. **Spindler** *is the chairman, he welcomes the audience to the Bolzano conference.*

Spindler   Good evening. Before we close things at the end of this third international conference on the Iceman in Bolzano, I want us to indulge in a little speculation after all the rigorous scientific debate of the last few days. And I want to ask the question, which is always asked of us involved in the investigation, what do we think he was actually doing up at 3,000 metres? So without further ado, let me reintroduce Professor Fitz from Zurich.

Fitz   Ja, danke, darf ich kurz wiederholen. Wir haben in Zürich den Dickarm des Eismannes untersucht und haben dabei einen ganz erstaunlichen Fund gemacht, und zwar haben wir im Stuhlgang Eier des Peitschenwurmes gefunden. Der Peitschenwurm ist ein Parasit der den Menschen vom Schwein her befällt. Somit muss es zur Zeit des Eismannes schon Hausschweine gegeben haben. Die hohe Zahl der Eier läßt darauf schliessen, dass wir uns in der Schweiz so häufig mit Parasiten beschäftigen . . . (*He laughs at his own joke.*)

Spindler   What he is saying is that the Iceman had, in his stomach, a worm . . . and that it was giving him some discomfort . . . and he's making a joke about it, it's a bit difficult to translate, it's a Swiss joke.

Fitz   Wir haben heute in den Tropen etwa acht Millionen Menschen die am Peitschenwurm erkrankt sind und Medikamente gibt es erst seit den sechziger Jahren.

He hands the microphone to the **Greek Delegate**.

Greek Delegate Αυτό ηου θέλω εγώ υα τουίοω είυαι ότι ο Iceman είχε μαξί του ένα χάλκινο τοεκούρι. Αυτό το οτοιχείο είναι οημαντικό διότλ . . . τι ουμβαίνει; What? Oh!

The other **Delegates** *indicate that the translation machine no longer works.*

Greek Delegate   Oh, I'm afraid the translator has broken. Well, I'll try in English. The Iceman had with him an axe made from local copper, Alpine copper and we found in the trichoanalysis . . . Professor, how do you say trichoanalysis?

Spindler   Analysis of the hair.

Greek Delegate   Thank you. We found a high level of copper and we also found that he had two organs black . . . er . . . the organs . . . which organs, you say? How you call them?

Spindler   Lungs?

Greek Delegate   The lungs, the organs, the lungs were black. Why were they black? Because he was smoking a lot of smoke. He was smoking a lot of smoke during the smelting of the copper, so he could be said to be a smelter, a collector and seller of copper and going from one side of the Alps to the other. And as a conclusion what I wanted to say is that he was up there because he was a businessman . . . I mean a Neolithic businessman, a commercial traveller of his time.

English Delegate   Now I've only got one word to say on the subject and that is transhumance. Now transhumance is, as we know, seasonal. So there is movement of the flock, from one area to another, such as from the low lands, the valley, in the winter up to the high mountains for the summer. This area is famous for transhumance of sheep and has been so for at least 5,000 years. Now I'm not saying for certain that they are sheep. They could be sheep, they could also be goats, sheep or goats, sheep and goats because sheep and goats get on together very well as a species. They are remarkably loving creatures which brings me to my point, basically I'm saying that he's a shepherd, thank you.

French Delegate   Merci. Alors on a trouvé que l'objet qu'il tenait dans son poing . . . était un antibiotique naturelle . . .

US Delegate   We can't understand you, I'm afraid.

French Delegate   Oh . . . well, I too will try in English. (*Pause.*) So, maybe he was a doctor. Thank you.

US Delegate   I've only one word to say and that is tassle. This is the only object which is on or about the Iceman which can be considered ornamental. It is a very beautiful iridescent marble bead. It is two point four centimetres in diameter and it has a hole in the middle. Now, this hole is threaded through with fur which has been knotted. What do these knots signify? I think they are clearly spiritual and, therefore, it is quite obvious that this man is some sort of shaman. It is very hard for us to understand what a shaman is today but we do have marble, so that's something. But to help us contextualize the idea of a shaman, in modern terms, we could even consider him as an early form of psychiatrist. It is not that ridiculous. If we are speculating, after all, we could imagine that he might have taken this marble bead and dangled it in front of the eyes of someone to try and hypnotize them. But actually, to be honest, what I'd rather discuss here today is the word violence. I'd like to talk about violence. Now this is a man, ladies and gentlemen, who leaves his village at a very inappropriate time with broken ribs. What the hell is he doing? We are talking about a patriarchal society, of course, I think the ladies in the audience will understand what I'm talking

about. I mean, where is his woman? Now it seems to me
that she is obviously not in his bed and I think we have a
classic case of Neolithic male egos in which he was forced
from his village as a result of . . .

She is cut off by the **French Delegate** *who takes the microphone.*

French Delegate   Si on parle de la violence, on doit bien
sûr penser que cet homme avait faim . . .

*The microphone is taken from her and it is again explained that the
translation is not working.*

English Delegate   It is no longer working . . .

US Delegate   Don't snatch that thing from her . . . now
this is exactly what I'm talking about, ladies and gentlemen.

French Delegate   Well. What can I say? This man was
in great trouble. Thank you.

US Delegate   Is that all you're going to say?

English Delegate   Cloud-cuckoo-land, I'm afraid. I
mean there is not one example of Neolithic violence which
leaves specific enough traces that we can truly speculate of
its exact form . . .

The microphone is taken by the next delegate.

Greek Delegate   No, no, my friend. There are carbon
deposits under many of the villages which suggest they have
been burned . . .

The microphone is taken by the next delegate.

Swiss Delegate   It is true that the Iceman had four
broken ribs but it is also true that he had a worm . . .

The microphone is taken by **Spindler**. *The* **Delegates** *continue to
argue among themselves. During* **Spindler**'s *speech the* **Delegates**
sink to the floor and then move steadily across stage.

Spindler   It is true that there is little empirical evidence as
to the form that violence took in the later Neolithic period.

Of course people fought one another, they always have.
Carbon deposits in Neolithic sites suggests that villages were
burned to the ground. We do not know how or why. But
there is one archaeological site that testifies to the exact
nature of violence in that period. A shocking example. In
Talheim in south-west Germany, in 1983, are the ruins of a
Neolithic village. On the edge of the village a mass grave
was discovered. More than half the individuals were lying
on their stomachs, their arms and legs sticking out in all
directions at absurd angles in defiance of anatomy. Each
one wedged on top of another. Everyone had been
murdered. Some of the blows had been administered while
the bodies were upright. Others while the dying were lying
on the ground. As there are no defensive fractures, one may
assume a regular execution. Afterwards the bodies were
carelessly tossed into a pit. The community of dead
represent the complete population rate of a Neolithic
village. Men, old men and women, children too. It is
conceivable that a fate similar to that of Talheim also befell
the Iceman's native village.

Spindler (*VO*)   In a hopeless situation he succeeded in
fleeing from the enemy . . .

Scene Thirty-four

Behind the plastic the light comes up on **Virgil** *standing next to his
bed, naked. As he speaks the bed moves away from him. The Iceman's
last moments merge with* **Virgil**'s *journey to his bed.*

Virgil (*VO*)   In a hopeless situation he succeeded in fleeing
from the enemy. Every effort was made to capture him. If,
as we know from Talheim, even women and children were
massacred, how much more dangerous would a grown
man's escape from the pogrom seem to the victors? His only
advantage was his superior local knowledge. There was no
hope of return at whatever time and for whatever purpose.
So the man set out in the direction of Hauslabjoch, hoping

that beyond the main ridge of the Alps he might escape his pursuers.

Over the following text, the chair slowly becomes the puppet of the Iceman. The rest of the company come around the table and take the puppet. It has a stick and its face is suggested by a towel. The puppet of the Iceman follows the final moments of the Iceman in his gully, 5,000 years ago.

Virgil (*VO*)   Evidently overtaken by a blizzard or sudden fog, the Iceman was in a state of total exhaustion. In the gully in the rock perhaps familiar to him from previous crossings of the pass, he sought what shelter he could from the bad weather. With his failing strength he settled down for the night. He deposited his axe on the ledge of a rock.

The Iceman leans against the bed.

Meanwhile, it had grown dark. It was snowing ceaselessly and an icy cold penetrated his clothes. A terrible fatigue engulfed his limbs.

He knew that to fall asleep meant death.

He staggered forward a few more steps.

He slipped and fell against a rock.

The birch-bark container fell from his hand; his cap fell off.

He falls to his knees, his head falls against the stone.

He only wanted a short rest but his need for sleep was stronger than his willpower. He laid his head on the rock. Soon his clothes froze to the rough ground. He was no longer aware that he was freezing to death.

The puppet by now is lying on the stone. The only movements are its final breaths. The company slowly retreat from the body. **Virgil***'s voice comes off VO and the audience should be aware that he is now speaking on the mobile phone to* **Alice***. Her face can be seen in the two-way mirror.*

Alice   So is that what happened?

Virgil   How can we possibly know? It's just one theory. A story. It's one way of going there, isn't it? A story. We need stories. Alice, tell me what happened.

Alice   I told you, I can't remember.

Virgil   It's OK. It's all right. Then imagine.

Alice   In the village there is an apple orchard. It's a sunny afternoon. And I find him asleep on the grass between the trees. One hand open on the grass, palm upwards, the other under his back. I can tell you everything about his face. I didn't wake him up. Virgil. Are you still there?

Virgil   Yes.

Alice   What are you wearing?

Virgil   What kind of question is that?

Alice   I just want to know.

Virgil   A T-shirt and trousers.

Alice   Do I know them?

Virgil   No . . .

Alice   Well, take them off.

Virgil   What?

Alice   Take them off.

Virgil   Why?

Alice   Why? Because I can see you.

Virgil   All right. I'll do it. Wait there. Don't go anywhere.

He takes off his clothes and gets on to the bed.

Virgil   Well, what do you want me to do now?

Alice   I just want you to talk to me. Tell me what you're doing.

Virgil   Well, that's easy enough because I'm just sitting on my bed . . .

The call starts to break up and we can no longer hear him.

Alice   You're beginning to break up . . .

Virgil   . . . and in a few minutes I'm going to make myself a . . .

Alice   Hello, hello . . . ? Hello, can you hear me? I don't know if you can hear me. If you can hear me, I'll go and see the Iceman tomorrow and tell you what he's like. And please ring me back. (*Pause.*) I'd like that.

Scene Thirty-five

Virgil *also realizes that they have been cut off. He once again sits on his bed. He gets up and looks in the mirror.* **Alice** *can still be seen behind it. When* **Alice***'s voice begins we should be uncertain for a moment whether it is in* her *mind or* **Virgil***'s.*

Alice (*VO*)   What does nakedness remind us of? Dear God, what does nakedness remind us of? Naked, our needs are so clear, our fears so natural.

Virgil *stands alone in front of the table in his room.*

Alice (*VO*)   There is nothing innocent about the naked. Only the newborn are innocent. Seeing a naked body of any age we remember our own, putting ourselves in someone else's place, in the gully, for example, 5,000 years ago.

He climbs on the table, evoking the dual image we have seen throughout the piece: when alone at the beginning; as the Iceman in the forensic lab; as himself imagining **Alice** *with the other man, the BBC correspondent.*

Seeing a naked body of another person we make an inventory of our own.

The other cast members appear silently behind the table and hold up the metal frame of the Iceman's refrigeration unit in front of them. They are looking at him in his museum in Bolzano. **Alice** *joins them. Through her VO we begin to understand they are looking at him not with mere ghoulish curiosity, not in horror, but with empathy.*

Shoulder blade, ribs, clavicle. We list the sensations we feel in each part, one by one, all of them indescribable, all of them familiar, all of them constituting a home.

Suddenly, strangely, one of the people behind the frame slips under it and continues towards the Iceman as if drawn into his presence. In one moment they have changed places. The man watching is on the table. He has put himself in the Iceman's place and the Iceman has become naked **Virgil** *again.*

Then, one by one, the members of the company follow each other in lying in the place of the Iceman. They lay themselves down and roll off again, just as generation succeeds generation in a never-ending cycle.

Virgil   All of them indescribable.

Alice   All of them indescribable.

Virgil   All of them familiar.

Alice   All of them familiar.

Virgil   All of them constituting a home.

Alice   All of them constituting a home.

Virgil   Constituting a home.

Alice   Constituting a home.

Virgil   A home.

Alice   A home.

The words echo. The rolling becomes quicker and quicker. The bed and the sink slide offstage as the image becomes concentrated on these continuously rolling, tumbling bodies. They are backlit now the entire width of the stage by neons and you can only see them in silhouette.

*Underneath which there are the repeating mantra-like voices of all the
company . . .*

Voices (*VO*)   A broken stick. Splinters of wood. Scraps of
leather. Strips of hide. Fur. Tufts of twisted grass. Fragments
of birch bark. Two round objects on a piece of twine.

*Finally the last company member rolls over the table. The table itself
hurtles offstage. The neons rise and clear. The company form a line
DS. They lean forward as if about to take a step. Their silhouettes
briefly evoke the photographs of Muybridge. From standing they lean
back as if assessing the size of a mountain in front of them. Suddenly
their heads snap sideways. What have they seen? The gully? A parent?
The future? The audience now becomes aware of a huge projection of
the Iceman, emerging on to the back plastic. The company turn towards
it. They walk US towards the body of the Iceman.*

Before they get there . . .

Fade to black.

Methuen Modern Plays

include work by

Jean Anouilh
John Arden
Margaretta D'Arcy
Peter Barnes
Sebastian Barry
Brendan Behan
Dermot Bolger
Edward Bond
Bertolt Brecht
Howard Brenton
Anthony Burgess
Simon Burke
Jim Cartwright
Caryl Churchill
Noël Coward
Lucinda Coxon
Sarah Daniels
Nick Darke
Nick Dear
Shelagh Delaney
David Edgar
David Eldridge
Dario Fo
Michael Frayn
John Godber
Paul Godfrey
David Greig
John Guare
Peter Handke
David Harrower
Jonathan Harvey
Iain Heggie
Declan Hughes
Terry Johnson
Sarah Kane
Charlotte Keatley
Barrie Keeffe
Howard Korder

Robert Lepage
Stephen Lowe
Doug Lucie
Martin McDonagh
John McGrath
Terrence McNally
David Mamet
Patrick Marber
Arthur Miller
Mtwa, Ngema & Simon
Tom Murphy
Phyllis Nagy
Peter Nichols
Joseph O'Connor
Joe Orton
Louise Page
Joe Pnehall
Luigi Pirandello
Stephen Poliakoff
Franca Rame
Mark Ravenhill
Philip Ridley
Reginald Rose
David Rudkin
Willy Russell
Jean-Paul Sartre
Sam Shepard
Wole Soyinka
Shelagh Stephenson
C. P. Taylor
Theatre de Complicite
Theatre Workshop
Sue Townsend
Judy Upton
Timberlake Wertenbaker
Roy Williams
Victoria Wood

Methuen Contemporary Dramatists
Include

Peter Barnes (three volumes)
Sebastian Barry
Edward Bond (six volumes)
Howard Brenton
   (two volumes
Richard Cameron
Jim Cartwright
Caryl Churchill (two volumes)
Sarah Daniels (two volumes)
Nick Darke
David Edgar (three volumes)
Ben Elton
Dario Fo (two volumes)
Michael Frayn (two volumes)
Paul Godfrey
John Guare
Peter Handke
Jonathan Harvey
Declan Hughes
Terry Johnson (two volumes)
Bernard-Marie Koltès
David Lan
Bryony Lavery
Doug Lucie
David Mamet (three volumes)

Martin McDonagh
Duncan McLean
Anthony Minghella
   (two volumes)
Tom Murphy (four volumes)
Phyllis Nagy
Anthony Nielsen
Philip Osment
Louise Page
Joe Penhall
Stephen Poliakoff
   (three volumes)
Christina Reid
Philip Ridley
Willy Russell
Ntozake Shange
Sam Shepard (two volumes)
Wole Soyinka (two volumes)
David Storey (three volumes)
Sue Townsend
Michel Vinaver (two volumes)
Michael Wilcox
David Wood (two volumes)
Victoria Wood

Methuen World Classics

include

Jean Anouilh (two volumes)
John Arden (two volumes)
Arden & D'Arcy
Brendan Behan
Aphra Behn
Bertolt Brecht (six volumes)
Büchner
Bulgakov
Calderón
Čapek
Anton Chekhov
Noël Coward (seven volumes)
Eduardo De Filippo
Max Frisch
John Galworthy
Gogol
Gorky
Harley Granville Barker
   (two volumes)
Henrik Ibsen (six volumes)
Lorca (three volumes)

Marivaux
Mustapha Matura
David Mercer (two volumes)
Arthur Miller (five volumes)
Molière
Musset
Peter Nichols (two volumes)
Clifford Oders
Joe Orton
A. W. Pinero
Luigi Pirandello
Terence Rattigan
   (two volumes)
W. Somerset Maughan
   (two volumes)
August Strindberg
   (three volumes)
J. M. Synge
Ramón del Valle-Inclán
Frank Wedekind
Oscar Wilde

Methuen Student Editions

Jean Anouilh	*Antigone*
John Arden	*Serjeant Musgrave's Dance*
Alan Ayckbourn	*Confusions*
Aphra Behn	*The Rover*
Edward Bond	*Lear*
Bertolt Brecht	*The Caucasian Chalk Circle*
	Life of Galileo
	Mother Courage and her Children
Anton Chekhov	*The Cherry Orchard*
Caryl Churchill	*Top Girls*
Shelagh Delaney	*A Taste of Honey*
John Galsworthy	*Strife*
Robert Holman	*Across Oka*
Henrik Ibsen	*A Doll's House*
Charlotte Keatley	*My Mother Said I Never Should*
Bernard Kops	*Dreams of Anne Frank*
Federico García Lorca	*Blood Wedding*
	(bilingual edition)
John Marston	*The Malcontent*
Willy Russel	*Blood Brothers*
Wole Soyinka	*Death and the King's Horseman*
August Strindberg	*The Father*
J. M. Synge	*The Playboy of the Western World*
Oscar Wilde	*The Importance of Being Earnest*
Tennessee Williams	*A Streetcar Named Desire*
	The Glass Menagerie
Timberlake Wertenbaker	*Our Country's Good*

For a complete catalogue of Methuen Drama titles
write to

Methuen Drama
215 Vauxhall Bridge Road
London Sw1V 1EJ

or you can visit our website at: